Darkest Secrets

of

MAKING A PITCH FOR FILM AND TELEVISION:

How You Can Get
a Studio Executive, Producer, Name Actor or Private Investor to Say "Yes" to Your Project

2nd Edition

by

TOM MARCOUX
Feature Film Producer, Director, Screenwriter, Actor

A QuickBreakthrough Publishing Edition

ISBN-13: 978-0615928692
ISBN-10: 0615928692

QuickBreakthrough Publishing is an imprint of Tom Marcoux Media, LLC. More copies are available from the publisher, Tom Marcoux Media, LLC. TomSuperCoach@gmail.com or visit www.TomSuperCoach.com or Tom's blog: www.BeHeardandBeTrusted.com.

This book was developed and written with care. Names and details were modified to respect privacy.

Disclaimer: No fiduciary relationship is created hereby between the reader and author or publisher. The author and publisher acknowledge that each person's situation is unique, and that readers have full responsibility to seek consultations with health, financial, spiritual and legal professionals. The author and publisher make no representations or warranties of any kind, and the author and publisher shall not be liable for any special, consequential or exemplary damages resulting, in whole or in part, from the reader's use of, or reliance upon, this material.

Dedication and Acknowledgements: Special thanks to the team that made this book possible. Thanks to the terrific author, book/film consultant and art director, Johanna E. Mac Leod for terrific insights. It is also dedicated to the other team members. Thanks to David MacDowell Blue, Sherry Lusk and Joan Harrison for editing. Thanks to Judita Bacinskaite for the book design. Thanks to Johanna E. Mac Leod for rendering the back cover. Thanks to my father, Al Marcoux, for his concern and efforts for me. Thanks to my mother, Sumiyo Marcoux, a kind, generous soul. Thanks to Rachael Masako Ing for rendering this book's front cover. Thanks to Johanna E. Mac Leod for the cover photography and the book cover concept of pitching the "your pitch" baseball. Thank you to Higher Power and our enthusiastic audiences and readers. The best to you.

Darkest Secrets of Making A Pitch for Film/Television:
"Learn how to get inside producers' heads and sell your story to Hollywood. This insightful book shows you how to zing a curveball right past the parts of the Hollywood exec's brain that want to say no before you even make your pitch. In these pages you will learn what works when pitching, and more importantly, why, so you can get to YES much more often. Buy this book now. Consider it Spring Training before the big game."—Danek S. Kaus, Produced Screenwriter; author of *Screenwriting for Authors*

"Tom Marcoux is one of the most persuasive people I know. He provides research-based methods so that you can get people to say "Yes!" to your project. Get this book–a Must Read. I have hired Tom as my media coach and I'm thrilled with the results I've gained." Dr. JoAnn Dahlkoetter, Olympic Sports Psychologist and #1 best-selling author of *Sports Psychology Coaching for Your Performing Edge*

Praise for Tom Marcoux's Previous Books in the Film/Television Series:
"*Darkest Secrets of the Film and Television Industry Every Actor Should Know* gives you the toolkit...from acting skills to self promotion! It shows you to avoid making seemingly small mistakes can prevent you from getting a role you know you are right for. It even teaches you how to produce a video for YouTube or webisodes. As an actress, I really value this. You, too, can become one of the savvy working actors. Read the book and use the information!"—Carole Wilkinson, actress

"Looking back on my experiences as a film maker, there are times I really could have used this book, ***Darkest Secrets of Film Directing.*** Easy to read, this book gives helpful tips and lessons for different situations you will encounter in your film career. One that really hit home was "Darkest Secret #4: People Will Get Angry. Deal With It." This section shows how people get upset on the set and how to deal with it. For any director, that's one of the hardest lessons to learn and anger on the set is a common situation. Definitely worth it!."—Daniel Buhlman, film director and actor

About Tom Marcoux as a Film Director and Actor:
"As a director, Tom consistently creates an environment where artists are encouraged to explore and discover the material, without compromising his own vision of the project. By allowing everyone to bring their best ideas to the table, Tom creates an environment that allows good work to thrive."—Dan Wilson, actor, playwright, director and producer

"Tom treats cast and crew with great respect. He listens to ideas, allows a lot of give and take. Tom is interested in seeing what others can bring to a project. His support helped me express the truth in my scenes."—David MacDowell Blue, actor, screenwriter and author of *The Annotated Carmilla*

"I strongly recommend Tom Marcoux as an actor. I have cast him in multiple projects, and he always comes through for me. Tom has great range as an actor. On the set, I have seen him express tears in one scene and later do a stand–up comedy improvisation."—Randi Acton, Casting Director

CONTENTS

BOOK 1

This is the book I wish existed when I began in the film industry. Do you have a movie you want to make? So did I. Or a screenplay that you want produced? Me, too. Are you going to pitch a project to a studio executive, producer, name actor or private investor? I've made many pitches. But back then I didn't know how and I hit wall after wall. It felt like a blow to the stomach at the time. In fact, I felt so much uncertainty and pain that I found myself avoiding the whole situation. I would stay up too late at night rewriting a screenplay, sleep all day, and lose that day when I needed to be out looking for funding. (Perhaps you can relate to that.)

The good news is you can avoid feeling stuck. Now, through this book, I will be your coach. Much of this material builds on my observations of dire mistakes, my own and others'. After successfully gaining funding for a number of projects and international distribution (one film went to the Cannes film market), I have compiled what worked.

I've seen other filmmakers give presentations that crashed and burned. So I'm inspired to provide you with the means to achieve your dream.

Pitching means asking producers, name actors, and studio executives to help you get your film made. Many filmmakers (particularly at the beginning of a career) enlist private investors for the money to make their movie. No one pretends this makes for an easy job. But remember, people do it all the time, successfully. You can as well. In the pages that follow you will learn the Darkest Secrets of this process—what traps and problems lie ahead. More, you'll find countermeasures that work. All those problems waiting for you? You can solve them. Traps can be avoided. Dangers are there to be nullified, just as bad habits or wrong assumptions wait for the chance to be broken. By you.

DARKEST SECRET #1: IT'S NOT WHAT YOU CLAIM, BUT WHAT YOU SHOW THAT COUNTS

Many filmmakers think making a great pitch is about the words—saying the right things. The perfect catch words, the exciting turn of phrase, the tag line that puts the whole thing into focus.

Let's look deeper. First, realize that when speaking, you use your neocortex, the part of your brain devoted to rational thinking. But when the studio executive listens, she uses her *reptile brain* to do it.

The neocortex deals with reason, logic, finding patterns. You use it in organizing your DVD collection or filling out a form.

When composing an email message, balancing your checkbook, installing software—the neocortex does what you need. A lot of formal education ends up designed to help train you in using that part of your brain.

But it isn't what you listen with. Our reptile brains don't analyze for the purpose of understanding nor doing an abstract calculation. Rather, that part of the stuff inside our skulls aims for a much more narrow agenda: Survival.

Closely related to the reptile brain is what we call the emotional brain. It too has a single, intense focus: Avoiding loss.

So already, you're in a situation of "disconnect." You're talking from the neocortex and they're listening from the reptile and emotional brains. Never forget a pitch consists of asking someone to take a risk, to put their money down on what cannot help but be a gamble. Odds are, that money will vanish forever. And on some level, they know that. As interested as they may be in taking part in the film making process, as willing as their conscious minds may be to give you a chance, their reptile and emotional brains view everything about you as a threat. Your task is to overcome that. *Show them something!*

I'll cover three scenarios.

Scenario 1: Pitch to a Name Actor

To pitch to a name actor and get him or her into your film, show a video. Prove that you're a good filmmaker. For example, twin brothers Logan and Noah Miller shot footage of baseball spring training in Tucson, Arizona. Next they used that footage to make a trailer for their feature film *Touching Home*, based on the true story of their relationship with their father. Then, they plotted what they called "the ambush," focusing on meeting Ed Harris, whom they wanted to portray the father.

Harris was to be honored at the San Francisco International Film Festival with a lifetime achievement award. The Miller twin brothers tried a number of different plans, but finally invited a festival team member to ask for two minutes of Harris' time. She agreed. When the time came, the Miller brothers showed Harris their film trailer. In that trailer he noticed Logan throwing well. Harris said, "Nice throw. That was you, wasn't it?"

"Yes, sir," Logan replied.

"See, I can tell you guys apart already . . . I used to be a catcher.

Like I told the guy onstage, I always dreamed of playing in the big leagues. Didn't make it as far as you though, only made it to college."

Soon Harris asked, "Do you boys have any actors attached?"

"Brad Dourif."

"Wow . . . You guys must be getting this out there. Brad Dourif is excellent, love his work," Harris said.

After a moment, Harris accepted their screenplay with their business card and a DVD of the trailer. Ultimately, Harris did accept the role and the film was made. Bravo, Miller twins!

Now, how does this all relate to the neocortex/reptile brain dilemma? In showing the trailer, the Miller twins bypassed an actor's reptile brain-concerns with survival. The subconscious thoughts related to the reptile brain might sound like: "Who are these kids? Making a movie with them would torpedo me in the industry."

Further, the trailer quieted the emotional brain, which might sound like: "Working on a tiny, independent film would cost me time and income. Also, this would disrupt my relationship with my agent."

Instead, the trailer excited the pleasure and memory centers of Harris' brain. The trailer created "wanting" in Harris' brain. Enough to accept the screenplay and read it. And that made the Miller twins' pitch successful.

Scenario 2: Pitch to a Potential Investor

If you have a name actor involved with your project, show a video in which he or she addresses the camera.

For example, producer "Susan Ohlee" has convinced a name actor to "attach" himself to her film *She Knows More*. Now Susan needs something better than merely saying to people, "I've got [name actor] attached."

Instead, Susan shows potential investors a video in which the name actor says, "Hi, I'm [name actor] and I'm on board with this film *She Knows More*. This is a great script, and I know that the director Susan Ohlee is really sharp and a good director. So I invite you to invest in this film. I'll see you at the wrap party!"

Do you see how much more power showing a video conveys? So much more personal than merely saying the words, "Oh, yeah. [Name actor] is involved with *She Knows More*."

Some readers will say, "But I don't have a name actor." Then, you lead with whatever impressive element you have. Show a video of a top scientist if your film is about cutting edge science. Show a video of one of your mentors praising your talent and diligent work. Such video testimonials will help you get to the next level. Perhaps at that level, your video testimonials will help you gain a name actor.

And we'll notice that a number of the most successful films had no name actors. Some genres attract higher box office earnings. One film jumps to mind: *Night of the Living Dead*, made for a $114,000 budget and earning $12 million domestically and $18 million internationally.

Scenario 3: Pitch to a Studio Executive

A screenwriter pitches her script and at some point says something like:

"...the tall man slams his fist straight into Mark's jaw. Mark crashes through the window! Nineteen stories up! But—he just manages to grab onto the ledge! There's broken glass everywhere. It cuts into his hands as he holds on for dear life! Blood oozes from the cuts."

The screenwriter is painting a *picture* in the executive's mind, making him *see* the action. This is known as creating a word picture. You might say, "Good idea." But what helps you the most is understanding why. Your goal is to get the executive to shift mental gears. Remember, he starts by listening with his reptile and emotional brains. No matter what he consciously thinks or believes, his nervous system categorizes you as a possible threat. You must arouse "curiosity and desire," that is, you want him (or her) to emotionally engage with your material. In fact, a top business pitch expert who has successfully raised tens of millions of dollars, Oren Klaff, makes exactly that point. In the end you arouse one of two sets of reactions: either "curiosity and desire" (which puts the listener on your side) or unfortunately you arouse "fear and dislike"—which makes for an unsuccessful pitch.

As we saw in the scenario with Ed Harris, viewing the trailer of the baseball spring training engaged him; his *curiosity and desire* were stimulated. His love of baseball helped intrigue him with the proposed film.

Writer–director–producer Jerry Zucker (director of the hit movie *Ghost*) once said, "In the movie business, people would much rather watch a 10–minute DVD than read a 120–page screenplay." So if you have a comedic screenplay, film part of it before an audience and be sure that microphones pick up the laughter from audience members! What does this do? It gets the studio executive to calm fears that the film may not get laughs. You're proving that the material works.

You have other options. You can film short films and place them on YouTube.com. For example, producer–director Sam Raimi (trilogy of *Spider-man* films) hired Uruguayan filmmaker Fede Alvarez as the director of the remake of Raimi's cult hit *The Evil* Dead based on the strength of Alvarez's low–budget YouTube hit short, *Panic Attack!* It's apparent that producer–director Sam Raimi found *Panic Attack!* intriguing; it aroused his curiosity and desire.

Points to Remember:

- **Darkest Secret #1: It's not what you claim, but what you show that counts.**

- **Your Countermeasure:**

Create some kind of film to engage and excite your target audience—an actor, executive, or private investor. Perhaps film a trailer, or a little scene from the script before a live audience, or a testimonial from a name actor interested in the film.

DARKEST SECRET #2: "NEEDINESS" GIVES OFF A SMELL—AND IT STINKS

You want to see your screenplay produced, or to get a movie deal. Maybe have a private investor pledge funds to help produce your film. Wanting is good. It starts the wheels turning, plans shaping, opportunities being created. On the other hand, desperately needing something can torpedo all your efforts. Sounds like a contradiction, doesn't it? But no—the difference between positive ambition and need can be subtle, but in pitching the effect ends up profound.

Positive ambition comes from a sense of purpose, an emotional place of self–confidence and with an enthusiasm you invite others to share. Neediness is an invitation to pity. It hints of fear, timidity, and a lack of will. Positive ambition inspires confidence. Neediness invokes contempt.

Why? People flinch around neediness. It bothers them. Maybe it reminds them too much of a time when they felt weak. Or perhaps they've had bad experiences in the past with those who manipulate through guilt. Many of us have. And they subconsciously feel that if you're desperate, maybe lots of others have seen through you and rejected you already.

You may, in fact, need to sell a screenplay to pay this month's rent. But the point is that you must *avoid coming across as needy*.

Many years ago, I had a friend who was running a conference. He knew that I had just started as a professional speaker and I wanted to address his conference audience. He rejected my application. My friend wanted only "established speakers who already had a following." It hurt. And I lost a lot of energy to feeling betrayed, which slowed me down.

Eventually, I took responsibility for my own thoughts and told myself: "This was one possibility. I'll look for many opportunities. I have something valuable to offer and the universe is a large place with many opportunities."

I share this story to illustrate that our thought patterns have power. A strong way to avoid coming across as needy is look on each meeting as one of many opportunities. On the other hand, anyone who looks on one particular meeting as a "one and only opportunity" will feel stressed out.

Along those lines, I invite you to look on each pitching opportunity as an "opportunity to practice." Tell yourself "I'll have many opportunities"—then you can relax a bit.

You can develop your own "many opportunities." Here's how a screenwriter can drop neediness. It's best to have three screenplays:

1. One screenplay that you're marketing.
2. One screenplay that you're finishing.
3. One screenplay that you're starting.

Why? So you won't be devastated if studio executives reject your finished screenplay. Secondly, studio executives often say, "What else have you got?" And you'll have two other projects to bring to their attention.

Having at least three screenplays does wonders for your own

well being. You feel stronger. Producer Linda Obst (*Contact* starring Jodie Foster and Matthew McConaughey and *Sleepless in Seattle* starring Tom Hanks and Meg Ryan) told me, "Have multiple projects. When one isn't [getting traction], toss it on the roof." Her "on the roof" comment was about keeping projects to the side, at the ready.

Having multiple projects gives you confidence and you can avoid the appearance of neediness.

Use *"want power"* and let go of *neediness*. By this I mean, "You want the person to say 'yes' to your project. But you do *not* need that particular person or that particular project to go forward. You have other options!"

Neediness is another word for desperation. Desperation is *not* attractive! What seems like desperation? Asking for validation with questions like: "So you like this project, right?" or "So this is what you're looking for, huh?" Also, desperate people's anguish is expressed with body language like: smiling too much, wringing hands, or leaning too far forward, hoping for the other person to "toss them a bone."

Your countermeasure to appearing needy is to build up your center of strength. You do that by focusing on empowering thoughts. Here are four elements:

1. Focus on the value you bring
Let's face it: There is no movie without a screenplay. A great film usually begins with a great screenplay. So if you're a screenwriter, you're bringing value (because, of course, you've written a good script!).

As a producer, you bring value when offering a film investment opportunity. The investor's money may just sit in some account. But when the investor has the opportunity to invest in your film, she is helping bring something good into the world. You even give her something to talk about at parties.

2. You are meeting the other person as a peer
Sure the other person may have higher social status or more money, but you share the same value as a fellow human being. And, according to pitch-master Oren Klaff, you can emphasize your "situational status." Your expertise and the unique details of your project is why everyone has gathered to hear your pitch. That's the basis of your situational status. Be sure to focus on the empowered attitude that you are "sharing something valuable" with the people assembled. That's when you become a peer. Everyone in the room puts something valuable on the table. Remember, you are the catalyst. When you pitch, you bring something new and valuable into the room.

3. You have the confidence that you're going to meet several people and you're offering the opportunity to do something exciting and profitable
It's an opportunity to be in business with you. Why? Because you have done your homework and have something valuable to offer. Whether you pitch to a studio executive, a name actor, a producer or a private investor, you already have a plan to meet a number of people. Why is that important? Because no one person holds your fate in his or her hands. You're going to talk to several people and then *you ultimately pick* who you'll work with—among those who express interest.

I tell myself before a meeting, "Let's find out who wants to play." After you find interested parties, think about who may be a match. Some people really would be a bad match with your offering. Meet them and move on to better prospects.

4. Keep your faith that the right people and right elements will fall into place
When you study case histories, you discover that projects met setback after setback after setback. Yet, the right people ultimately came together. Big projects or small, business or art or educational, engineering or sports—it happens. Time and again.

Producer Brian Grazer brought his film project, a romantic comedy about a man, a mermaid and modern–day Manhattan, to studios for eight years. And personnel at all the studios rejected the project. By the time he returned to Disney, the company was starting up a new division, Touchstone Pictures, and then—and only then—did *Splash* find a home as the first film released by Touchstone Pictures!

Keep your faith. Realize that things keep changing, new trends start becoming popular, friends get new jobs, and rivals move away or fade away.

Getting things done requires time and persistence. For example, David Webb Peoples wrote a screenplay, *The William Munny Killings*, in 1976. Clint Eastwood purchased it in 1979 but waited until 1991 to film the screenplay as *Unforgiven*. The film won four Oscars: Best Picture, Best Director (Clint Eastwood), Best Supporting Actor (Gene Hackman) and Best Editing (Joel Cox). It was nominated for five other awards, including Eastwood as Best Actor. Peoples won L.A. Film Critics and National Society of Film Critics awards for best screenplay.

During the long wait before *Unforgiven* came to fruition, Peoples wrote numerous other screenplays—many were produced and he even directed a feature film based on one.

Keep your faith—and that requires self–discipline. You must focus on empowered thoughts. Some people like to focus on affirmations—statements that are personal, present tense and positive. Here's an affirmation: "I am selling a screenplay today." Some people report affirmations help a lot. Other people say, "Affirmations don't work for me because part of me feels that I'm lying to myself."

Instead, I prefer asking empowering questions and providing myself with answers. This process swiftly changes the direction of my thoughts.
Here are sample questions:

1. Why is my film a real opportunity for investors?
2. Why am I a good person to be in business with?

3. What good value do I bring to this meeting?
4. Why will they enjoy saying "yes" to my film?

Here are examples of answers that filmmakers provide:

1. Why is my film a real opportunity for investors?
Because we're focusing on a proven demographic that attends movie theaters: African Americans looking for a comedy related to their own experiences.

2. Why am I a good person to be in business with?
Because I'm trustworthy. I meet deadlines. I think through situations. I collaborate well.

3. What good value do I bring to this meeting?
I'm bringing a screenplay that is compelling. The story catches you and doesn't let go.

4. Why will they enjoy saying "yes" to my film?
Because this film has both quality and value in the marketplace . . .

Use the above questions and your own answers to strengthen your resolve. Then you will naturally avoid the appearance of neediness. If you feel any hesitation, do your homework. Improve the elements of your project. Build your confidence on the rock of value. Go forth and share value.

Points to Remember:

- **Darkest Secret #2: "Neediness" gives off a smell—and it stinks.**

- **Your Countermeasure:**

Empower yourself. Focus on the value you bring to the studio executive, producer, name actor or private investor. Plan in advance to meet with many people to find the right match. Do your homework with respect to these elements:

1. *Focus on the value you bring.*
2. *You are meeting the other person as a peer.*
3. *You have the confidence that you're going to meet several people and you're offering the opportunity to do something exciting and profitable.*
4. *Keep your faith that the right people and right elements will fall into place.*

DARKEST SECRET #3: CONFIDENCE ATTRACTS, ARROGANCE REPELS

Why does confidence attract? Because the reptile brain focuses on survival. If the pitch–maker comes across as confident, then the listener feels like he's in good hands. This translates to "a good project leader means we'll survive here." Remember, the listener takes in the pitch through the filters of the reptile brain and emotional brain. The reptile brain constantly targets survival. For the studio executive, choosing viable projects equals job survival. For the producer, choosing appropriate screenplays means living another day to produce the next movie. Private investors have various motives; one can include being able to justify to a spouse the reasons for investing in a movie that may result in a loss.

If the one giving the pitch seems *not* to be confident, then the reptile brain quickly has thoughts like: "This guy does not believe in his own project" or "Something feels wrong here" or—ultimately—"I'll get hurt by investing in this."

It's best to avoid appearing doubtful or nervous. But just as deadly to all your dreams is the opposite. Lack of confidence destroys. So does arrogance. If you go too far and express arrogance, the listener is repelled. Why? Arrogance can often make the listener angry. Before we go further about anger, here's how *The Merriam–Webster Dictionary* defines *arrogance*: "an attitude of superiority manifested in an overbearing manner or in presumptuous claims or assumptions."

All four elements incite anger. Let's explore them:

1. Attitude of superiority . . . the listener thinks "Who the hell does he think he is?"
2. Overbearing manners . . . the listener thinks: "How dare he! I demand respect."
3. Presumptuous claims . . . the listener thinks: "No. That's wrong. This guy's film is *not* that 'fresh and original.'"
4. Presumptuous assumptions . . . the listener thinks: "All this guy is doing is showing how narrow–minded and uninformed he is. And he's getting on my nerves!"

A number of arrogant people also demonstrate lack of patience. Stanford University professor and author of *Power: Why Some People Have It—And Others Don't*, Jeffrey Pfeffer notes: "Losing patience causes people to lose control and offend others, and that can cost them their jobs [or a deal]." He also notes that people in a power mind-set "engage in all kinds of disrespectful and rude behavior."

So what does arrogance sound like? Here are some examples:

1. "Because I was a cop. I know how to make this movie." (A listener may feel that the individual has some useful experience, but he lacks film–industry specific knowledge.)
2. "Now listen here. The right way to do this is . . ."
3. "I know that movie–goers need the story dumbed down. All they need is enough car chases and explosions . . ."

Earlier, I mentioned that arrogance often incites anger. Let's go deeper. Anger is often a response to subconscious fear. Some subconscious thoughts may be:

- He's arrogant. What's he hiding?

- He's overdoing this. What's he trying to push me into? How can I get hurt?
- This jerk is full of himself. He will be a nightmare to work with. It's better to kill this deal now!

Anger often arises because you feel that someone is trying to take over your life and to take what is yours. If someone is overbearing, what are they taking? Your feeling of self-esteem. So it becomes clear that showing arrogance can torpedo your pitch.

Instead, let's work our way toward a solution. Show confidence. One way to do that is to enrapture the listener as you tell a story. Here's something powerful about telling a story. You get the listener's brain chemistry on your side. Brain researchers have noticed our brains secrete the neurotransmitter dopamine when we anticipate a reward. How is telling a story giving the listener a surge of dopamine? First, when you tell an original story you're providing something new. Dr. Greg Burns, author of *Satisfaction,* notes, "How do you get more dopamine flowing in your brain? NOVELTY."

And what will be the reward? The end of the story. The fulfillment of our curiosity. As a professional speaker, I use a story to make a lasting impact for any point I'm making. Let's say I'm talking about how I value collaboration. I'll tell a story like:

"One of my strengths is I gather a team that can quickly improve the work. I always remember how Francis Ford Coppola was backed into a wall while directing *The Godfather*. Every day he's concerned that he might get fired. He knows that he needs a powerful scene in which the Godfather (that's Marlon Brando) needs to hand over the reins of the family business to his son, portrayed by Al Pacino. But Coppola does not have the time to write the scene. He's busy putting out fires. He calls up his friend Robert Towne, and Towne writes the scene. And the scene is excellent. The handing over of power. But more. You can see the love of father for son. And son for father.

And that's something that means a lot to me. Over the years, I have developed a circle of collaborators who I can call up and quickly improve whatever I'm working on . . ."

You probably noticed how I used certain details to *create tension* in the story:

- "Coppola was backed into a wall."
- "Every day he's concerned that he might get fired."
- "Coppola does *not* have the time to write the scene. He's busy putting out fires."

Let's go further. The confident person who delivers a pitch has designed and rehearsed the pitch to further create that ideal brain chemistry in the listener. Master pitch-maker Oren Klaff wrote: "Dopamine is the neurotransmitter of desire. Norepinephrine is the neurotransmitter of *tension*. Together they add up to *attention*."

Here's where confidence really comes into play. You become a master pitch–maker when you get the listener (studio executive, producer, name actor or private investor) to feel some tension. How do you do that? You exude confidence that you're bringing something valuable to their attention—and that you might take it away. This is the opposite of coming in groveling and needy.

Let's look at three scenarios:

Scenario 1: Pitch to a Private Investor

Susan (the pitch-maker) says, "I'm looking for people to do business with. Let's see if we're a match—if you're a match for this film investment opportunity."

Scenario 2: Pitch to a Studio Executive

Joseph, a screenwriter, tells himself: "I've worked real hard on this screenplay. I've hired great editors to make it excellent. I'm sure a number of people will want this screenplay. I'm looking for the right match, the right terms and a great fee." These internal thoughts give Joseph an edge because his attitude and body posture communicate that the screenplay is valuable. And he's confident about that!

Scenario 3: Pitch to a Name Actor

At some point, if Producer Cindy feels the time is right, she might say, "I'm not sure here. You may not be a fit for this role. Then, maybe we could work on something else in the future." The name actor will hopefully reply with something like: "Wait a minute. Let's talk some more about this. I think I'm going to do good things with this role."

All of the above words need to be expressed with an appropriate tone—a tone of comfort and confidence. Avoid a tone of "I'm special" (which would be associated with arrogance).

Let's face it. We walk a fine line between confidence and arrogance. Unfortunately, without a lot of practice and rehearsal, people tend to swing like a pendulum. They may appear "overconfident" or arrogant. Or they appear hesitant or nervous.

Instead, just show your comfort and belief in yourself and your project. Show that you're meeting the person like a peer. This is called *situational status* (which I mentioned earlier). You're bringing something of value to the situation. When you leave the room, the other person may have more power and wealth than you do, but in the moment, you're the one with the project and the expertise. Enjoy it. As I mentioned before, I have a phrase in my mind, "Let's see if they want to play." This particular phrase helps me relax.

Build your confidence on this premise: People who are good at what they do know it. Why? They've worked hard to develop their skills. And this leads us to two things that arrogant people often fail to do: rehearse and get coaching. Simply stated: it is arrogant to think that one can merely "wing it."

And the big thing for confidence is: rehearse, rehearse, rehearse.

I advise my clients and graduate students: Rehearse for at least 9 minutes a day. Anytime you feel nervous: Rehearse. You can call your answering system and rehearse using your cell phone. Or call a friend. Don't cram your rehearsal into one last day session for three hours. Instead, when you rehearse for 9 minutes, your subconscious mind works on the pitch the rest of the day.

I often do my rehearsal as the first thing of the day. I call it: *Worst first*. Authors, including Brian Tracy, note that the task that will give you the best results is probably the one you dread. So get it over early in the day! The rest of the day will flow easier. Build your confidence. Rehearse. Record your rehearsals. And it would help to get a speech/pitch coach (you can find me at www.BeHeardandBeTrusted.com).

You've worked hard developing your project. Now work on your pitch. Then you'll develop real confidence. It's worth it.

Points to Remember:

- **Darkest Secret #3: Confidence attracts, arrogance repels.**

- **Your Countermeasure:**

Design your pitch to provide desire and tension (to stimulate the brain to secrete neuron–transmitters dopamine and norepinephrine). Build your confidence: rehearse, rehearse, and rehearse.

DARKEST SECRET #4: GRAB THEIR ATTENTION OR CRASH AND BURN

Why is it so hard to grab someone's attention? Because their mind races at 500 words a minute. People only talk at 80–100 words a minute. So already you're competing with around 420 words of "noise" that may block your message.

So start with this idea: Your listener's mind is somewhere else until you compel the person to focus on you. How can you do that? You use a well chosen *frame*. As cognitive scientist George Lakoff writes: "Frames are among the cognitive structures we think with. For example, when you read a murder mystery, there is a typical frame with various kinds of characters: the murderer, victim or victims, possible accomplices, suspects, a motive, a murder weapon, a detective, clues."

So what does this mean? The way to get someone's attention is to give them what the brain uses all the time—a compelling *frame*, which is a cognitive structure that shapes our impression of the world. Imagine the physical frame placed around a painting. As artists know, the frame can highlight and augment the beauty of the paint.

Let's take this a step further. When a film director frames a shot, she is leaving some details out—for example, when she has a close-up on an actor's face.

Here's another way to think of a frame. It is something that leaves details out and focuses the viewer attention on specific elements.

A well–used frame *attracts the person's attention*. This process of attraction feels compelling to the listener. It's also better than a novice pitch–maker getting caught up in old ideas about selling: pushing an idea, educating a person to see the value of your product, and overcoming objections.

It helps to realize that you often face a competing frame when you're pitching. Remember, those 420 words of noise you're up against?—they often include the listener's *power frame*. The listener feels that he or she has the power: the ability to say "yes" or "no" to your project. The power frame is strong, and the listener may disrupt you with invasive questions, perhaps entertaining himself with your discomfort.

How do you overcome the power frame? Use what pitch–master Oren Klaff calls the "*intrigue frame*." Seize their attention. Use an intriguing story. Why is a story helpful here? It's how our brains are conditioned to take in input. Earlier, I talked about stimulating the ideal brain chemistry, that is, you want the neurotransmitters of dopamine (desire) and norepinephrine (tension) to release in your listener's brain. How do you do that? With a story. Cognitive scientist George Lakoff talks about the power of a *narrative*. There are cultural narratives like *Live Fast, Die Young* which people assign to the lives of James Dean, Marilyn Monroe and Janis Joplin. Lakoff notes that typical roles in a narrative are Hero, Helper, Villain and Victim.

Let's say I was pitching to a private investor and I notice that she's tapping her pen, which is disrupting my concentration. Here's something I'd use as a story (employing the intrigue frame):

"Cheryl, I noticed you tapping your pen. That reminds me of the time I was directing a feature film before 911.

Because it's prior to 911, we had access to a runway of this airport. And the shot called for a small plane's wing to go over my cameraman's head. But he was standing too tall. I knew that if I called out to him, he'd just turn his head and still get *hit* in the head! So I ran toward him and—"

Now, I have Cheryl's attention. I'm stimulating the ideal brain chemistry of the neurotransmitters of dopamine (desire) and norepinephrine (tension) to be released in Cheryl's brain.

At this point, you may wonder: "What does this have to do with my actual pitch?" Part of a good pitching strategy is to think through how you will seize the listener's attention if she is distracted. So I may transition from my airplane wing–cameraman story to how volatile the marketplace is and how I'm always vigilant whether I'm on the set or developing a movie franchise.

Let's go back to the actual story. Notice how I'm using Lakoff's typical roles in a *narrative* of Hero, Helper, Villain and Victim:

Victim (potentially): My cameraman
Villain: Wing of the small plane
Hero (potentially): Me.

Here's another example that Joel Bauer shares in his book *How to Persuade People Who Don't Want to Be Persuaded: Get What You Want Every Time*. Bauer was talking to a prospective client in her office. She was a manager, and she didn't see any value in Bauer being the spokesperson at her tradeshow booth. He had to break her thinking pattern [which was related to her *power frame* of "I know what won't work for my booth!"]. When Bauer noticed a rubber band encircling her wrist, he asked her to place it across her upper lip. The rubber band was cool to the touch. He asked her to stretch the rubber band and place it back on her lip. Now, the rubber band was warm to the touch. Bauer explained that in the same way, he heats up an audience at a tradeshow. Her prospective customers would tune in to his presentation.

"My crowds will pull in more early–adopters than you've ever had, precisely because my crowds are so big, so excited, so full of energy. A crowd draws a larger crowd!" Bauer explained to the manager. He had successfully seized the manager's attention and gained a contract.

Again, the idea here is to *intrigue* the listener. That's using the *intrigue frame*. Bauer took this one step higher by making the manager part of the story.

I do the same thing when I'm coaching a client and I'm demonstrating how to answer a tough question. I have the client stand up and slowly aim a punch toward my face. I block in the traditional karate style. Forearm meets forearm. I ask, "So what happens here?"

"You're blocking," my client says.
"Yes. And, *pain*! This is when force meets force," I say.

Then I have the client again slowly punch toward my face. This time I step out of the way and grab the punching arm using an *aikido* movement. I guide the client.

"This is *aikido*. See how I'm guiding you. That's how you handle a tough question . . ."

Again, this is all about intriguing the listener. Remember that an intrigue frame can overcome a power frame. Construct your intrigue frame out of a narrative. Use typical roles in a *narrative* of Hero, Helper, Villain and Victim.

Seize the listener's attention. If you don't, your pitch will crash and burn. Why? Because there is already 420 words racing in the listener's mind that compete with your presentation.

By the way, here is a frame that investors like: "We have an unfair advantage." That is, you've designed your film project to take advantage of certain openings in the marketplace. Investors like to be smart. Let them feel that way!

Points to Remember:

- **Darkest Secret #4: Grab their attention or crash and burn.**

- **Your Countermeasure:**

Be sure to design your pitch with frames and narratives in mind. Attract the listener to you by placing yourself in an intriguing story. Figure out what role (Hero, Helper, Villain, Victim) will seize the listener's attention.

DARKEST SECRET #5: PEOPLE DECIDE QUICKLY, BASED ON LITTLE INFORMATION

In his classic book *Blink,* Malcolm Gladwell noticed that people made quick, intuitive decisions. More, they based these decisions on something he referred to a "thin-slicing." Of all the information available, Gladwell observed, people took just a "thin–slice" of that information. Then they made a quick decision—one that settled in and wasn't going anywhere.

Near the end of the book, Gladwell wrote of unfair decisions made when people audition for orchestras. If the selection committee saw that a woodwind player was a woman, they tended to reject her application. Perhaps they based the rejection on the supposition that a woman with a smaller frame has less lung capacity. Gladwell also described a solution: Have all auditions take place with a screen between the musician and the selection committee, so the musician's gender would not enter the equation. This process would be truly fair for the selection of orchestra players.

Why am I sharing this material with you? Because those folks you're pitching to do the same thing. When pitching, you're up against that human habit to thin–slice and make a quick, permanent decision. As every pitch begins, unconscious judgments bubble up in the listener's mind. *He's nervous, probably trying to put one over on me.*

Look at the way this guy is dressed! She looks weak. Wait—what did they just say? Are they kidding me? This one doesn't know the answers to any questions! That nervous tick—he's hiding something.

Of course what you hope for—what you should be aiming for—are different snap judgments. *I like him. She sounds confident. I bet this will be a valuable project. He looks me in the eye, so he's honest. She knows what she's talking about. That's a good joke, this person understands humor! Wow, she didn't even blink—she is calm and forthright.*

Gladwell referred to a term for such instant judgments and quick decision–making. He called it *rapid cognition*. It helps to remember that rapid cognition is the listeners' tendency to make quick, permanent judgments based on very little data.

So stack things in your favor. Earlier, I've shared how listeners first interpret your pitch with the reptile brain (focused on survival) and the emotional brain (focused on preventing a loss). It's like these two brains guard the gate before your pitch eventually gets to the neocortex (site of all rational thinking). Avoid getting sucked into addressing the listener's neocortex and being detoured into gushing a bunch of analytical facts and figures at the beginning of your pitch. (Save that for later.)

A similar process pops up in job interviews. Interviewers look for a "red flag"—anything that reads as cause to reject an applicant. In recent years, interviewers scoured Facebook looking for photos of applicants at parties, drink in hand. Their bias showed against anyone presumed to be a heavy partier, one who finds it hard to wake up in the morning. Auditions can work the same way. At a "cattle call" with a lot of actors trying out, directors often first look for a reason to reject someone, just to reduce the pile of resumes to a manageable size! That is why many actors only list their age ranges, not a specific number. Far too easy for a 25–year–old to lose their chance because the character is twenty–three!

So the reptile brain and emotional brain automatically look for red flags. How can you overcome that? Develop in the listener what Dr. Robert Zajonc called "wanting." When you get the listener to *want* to do business with you and to *want* your project, you're succeeding. You're on your way to get a "yes" to your project.

Never try to fight the system the brain uses to defend itself. That way lies failure. Success on the other hand rests in your skill at using the brain's defenses. Remember rapid cognition? The way people tend to make instant, permanent decisions based on little actual knowledge? Now, we'll discuss a rapid cognition that's in your favor: *Hot Cognition*.

Hot Cognition is the opposite of the slow, cerebral, analytical "cold cognition." That is what scientists and historians do as part of their jobs. Your job is sales and entertainment. Make no mistake—Hot Cognition is indeed a form of rapid cognition. But it works in your favor! Pitch-master Oren Klaff may have put it best: "Deciding that you like something before you fully understand it—that's a Hot Cognition."

First, show confidence and seize the listener's attention. Klaff uses what he calls the "four frame hot cognition stack." He names the four "Intrigue, Prize, Time, and Moral Authority."

Before I describe the four in terms of a pitch, let's revisit the term *frame*. A frame is a cognitive structure we think with. It shapes our impression of the world. When a film director frames a shot, she is leaving some details out—for example when she has a close-up on an actor's face. Here's another way to think of a frame. It is something that leaves details out and *focuses* the viewer's attention on *specific* elements.

Scenario: Producer Pitches to a Studio Executive

1. The intrigue frame
You use a story to capture the listener's attention. You build it on a *narrative* made of typical roles: Hero, Helper, Villain and Victim. Imagine a producer "Jack" addressing a studio executive. "This film reminds me of when I was as a sniper in Afghanistan," Jack says. As you can see, Jack's words are intriguing. The studio executive wants to hear the rest of the story.

2. The prize frame
Pitch–makers often get caught up in their anxiety to win a "yes" from a studio executive, producer, name actor or investor. Stop. *Reverse* that. Demonstrate how you and your project are the real "prize." Jack says, "So I'm looking to get in business with a studio that wants a double punch: Both a thriller and a strong story. This can be a prestige picture that gets Oscar nominations. We're beginning well with an Oscar-winning screenwriter. So tell me again, how you guys would be a match for this project?" The situation is *switched*. Instead of the producer being desperate for a "yes" answer, this producer is getting the studio executive to chase him and the project. They become the "prize."

3. The time frame
People often go into action when they feel the clock ticking—some sort of time pressure. It takes finesse to use a time frame. Make a clumsy attempt and the listener might think, "You're not the boss of me, go away and good luck!" Let's notice that the time frame is the *third* layer of the *four frame hot cognition stack*. You make sure to create intrigue and rapport first.

So Jack has the studio executive already *wanting* his film project. Jack continues, "This is sounding good so far. I can hear it in your voice, Nina. You'd work hard to make this a great picture. And I have to let you know that I'll need to hear from you guys by Friday. Because on Monday, I'm scheduled with Joe ___ at Paramount and Susan ___ at Warners."

Using the time frame requires that you use a good tone in your voice. You also see how Jack was praising Nina, the studio executive. And by saying "I have to let you know," Jack tempers "the bad news." If you use a time frame, do so with caution.

4. The moral authority frame

This is the fourth layer of the *four frame hot cognition stack* with good reason. It's tricky to use this one well. And using the Moral Authority frame effectively depends on the rapport you've created and how much you've already inspired *wanting* in the listener. One method is to *use something the listener said* as a springboard. Nina says somewhere in the conversation, "My father served in the Gulf War. That's why I'm interested in your project."

Later in the conversation, Jack can say, "It means a lot to me. Your father served so you know what that means. And this film can be a great expression to vets of 'Thank you for your service to our fine country.'"

This is invoking the Moral Authority frame. This process involves delicacy because an error could make such wording sound like emotional blackmail. So you need to carefully craft your pitch and to rehearse it before a number of people to hear their reactions. Often, a pitchmaker is so enraptured with a project that they might not anticipate how someone could take a detail "the wrong way." Get some coaching. (You can find me via www.BeHeardandBeTrusted.com)

By using the four frame hot cognition stack, Producer Jack avoids coming from neediness. He has thought through the elements of his pitch and has found ways to make himself and the project *attractive*.

Again, the idea is to stimulate "wanting" in the listener.

Points to Remember:

- **Darkest Secret #5: People decide quickly, based on little information.**

- **Your Countermeasure:**

Be sure to tailor your pitch so that the listener's tendency to make a quick decision is based on "wanting" you and your project. You focus on getting the favorable "hot cognition," which is deciding that you like something before you fully understand it. When possible, develop a pitch using four frames (Intrigue, Prize, Time and Moral Authority).

DARKEST SECRET #6: SHOW FEAR AND YOU ARE FRIED

What are you afraid of? Not getting the deal. Perhaps not getting your film funded by private investors. Yes, there are plenty of other fears. But we'll focus on fears related to pitching.

Fear is connected to how much you need the deal. Oren Klaff wrote: "Neediness is a signal of threat. If you display neediness, it is perceived as just the kind of threat that the crocodile [reptile] brain wants to avoid. Neediness results in avoidance [by the listener]."

Show fear and you get a "no" answer from the studio executive, producer, name actor or private investor. On a deep level, what are we afraid of? Rejection and disappointment. So what mistakes do many of us make? We try to calm ourselves down by saying something to get an admission from the listener that they like us and like our project. We're looking for validation. Do NOT say or do anything seeking validation.

Here are Powerful Ways to Deal With Fear:

1. Mental focus

I like Oren Klaff's mantra: "I don't need these people. They need me. I'm the prize." Remember, if you're in the room, the listeners need something from you. That makes you and your project the prize. Some years ago, I negotiated with a distribution company for one of my feature films. One idea that helped me was *"If they're talking to you, you have more power than you think."* When the distribution company representative gave me their "standard distribution agreement," I went home, took out an audio recorder and identified 37 points I did not agree with. To even imagine that I could push the representative to accept any changes, I had to remind myself over and over: *"If they're talking to you, you have more power than you think."* I went back to the representative and gained changes to the contract for about 91% of the items.

2. Action

Often we take action in a subconscious manner. We may frown, tap a pen on the table or put our hands in our pockets while we give a presentation. These actions convey nervousness and self-doubt. Stop that.

How? Observe your actions. Rehearse and have a speech/ pitch coach point out how and when you look nervous. Here's an important habit to break: The novice pitch–maker will say something like: "So it's a good deal, right?" That's asking for validation and it reeks of self-doubt.

Rather, break this habit by developing a new, good one in its stead. After you complete your presentation *sit down, keep good posture, and have a small smile*. Why? Those three physical actions convey that you feel good about your presentation and that you're confident in yourself and your project.

Focus on *replacement actions*. Why? Because if you simply try to eliminate a bad habit, you leave a hole in your behavior pattern. That's the reason I'm being specific about the three above actions to take immediately after your pitch.

3. Show no behaviors asking for validation

What is validation? Dr. Steven Stosny writes about how validation is connected to the approval of others. What is that like? In the moment, "Sam" does not feel whole and worthwhile. So he looks to others to "prove" that he is right in his thoughts and feelings.

How do we ask for validation? It sounds like this: "So you can see that this is a great idea for a movie, huh?" We ask questions that sound like supplications. On a subconscious level, it like we're asking: "Please don't hurt me by saying no. Please show me a sign that I did well in my pitch." No! Do *not* let yourself fall into that default behavior. That's the kind of behavior that children demonstrate toward parents.

One solution is to use a process that many actors employ. Decide upon the appropriate thoughts to focus on. Then your behavior flows naturally. Focus on thoughts like: "I'm bringing something valuable to the table" or "I'm sharing an opportunity with them."

My favorite way to deal with fear is my pattern "Stay strong. Work your plan."

For example, at the moment, my team and I are preparing to launch a book *Crystal Pegasus* (the first in a series of children's books). Soon, I'll be pitching this series to producers, investors, studio executives—just like I've been talking about so far. I envision *Crystal Pegasus* as a trilogy of animated feature films or a TV series.

Let's say in a particular pitch, it looks like a studio executive is not going to decide in my favor. I will *not* let that knock me down. How? First, I'm prepared to make many pitches to potential people to find a great match. Second, I already have a plan: *Keep building the brand*. By that I mean, my team and I will keep moving forward (regardless of how many pitches) in our work for the next two books in the first trilogy of *Crystal Pegasus*. We move forward with plans for T-shirts and toys and more. For each subsequent pitch, I know that the Crystal Pegasus *brand will be stronger and more attractive*.

Earlier, I wrote about fear as related to how much you *need* a deal. Imagine that my *Crystal Pegasus* books and toys are doing well—then I will *not* need a particular deal. That's a position of strength. (If you're thinking that you don't have a franchise in mind, note the methods I provide for the screenwriter below.)

At this time, let's go further about eliminating neediness. Oren Klaff wrote: "The three rules of eradicating neediness [are]:
1. *Eliminate your desires.* It's not necessary to want things. Sometimes you have to let them come to you.
2. *Be excellent in the presence of others.* Show people one thing that you are very good at.
3. *Withdraw.* At a crucial moment, when people are expecting you come after them, pull away."

Let's begin with *"Rule #1." For many of us the three words "eliminate your desires"* sounds impossible. Of course, if you've written a screenplay, you want a deal and to have your screenplay made into a feature film.

Here's what helps: nonattachment. For more than a decade, I continue to teach a college course in Comparative Religion. Each semester, I share useful ideas about *nonattachment*. Let's begin with the experience of feeling attached to something. We start with an idea of "what we think should happen" or "what we desperately want to happen." That's attachment. It's like we're chained to an idea. And if we don't get what we want, it's easy to feel horrible.

In essence, when you're attached to something, you're practically *demanding* that the universe give you what you want on your personal timetable. It's a sure recipe to feel frustrated, disappointed—and some people report feeling depressed.

Isn't there a remedy for avoiding this much pain? Yes. Nonattachment. First, let's dispel a counterproductive notion. Nonattachment does NOT equal having no feelings or not caring at all. Sure you care. But you dial it down. How? You convert a *want* (or desire) into a *preference*. The first step is to *open your awareness* that for any situation there are *many* possible positive outcomes. Next, you declare yourself *open* to appreciate many of these positive outcomes.

How does this work? Let's say Miranda wants Steven Spielberg's company to buy her screenplay for $2.5 million. *Practicing nonattachment, she looks at the wide field of possible positive outcomes.* Perhaps, Disney will buy her screenplay at $450,000 and the film becomes a hit and she gets a percentage plus the immediate deal to write the sequel.

It takes effort for Miranda to go from "Oooh! I want the Spielberg deal!" to "I'll welcome some positive outcome." Here's an another thought. Miranda does *not* know what later positive outcomes can *build* on today's situation. For example, Brian Grazer felt deeply frustrated that his film project *Splash* met with rejection after rejection over eight years. But at a certain point, Grazer gained Ron Howard as the director for the film. *Splash* proved to be a hit film. Just two years later, Grazer and Howard founded Imagine Entertainment which has released numerous hit films including *Liar, Liar* (Jim Carrey), *The Nutty Professor* (Eddie Murphy), *The Da Vinci Code* (Tom Hanks) and many more.

It's possible that Miranda even sells her screenplay for $150,000 but begins a successful collaboration with a director that brings later unexpected good fortune.

Practicing nonattachment lightens Miranda's emotional load. Again, change what you want (a demand) into a *preference.* Perhaps, even tell yourself, "There are many possible positive outcomes here." This is a process of reducing your emotional investment in one particular idea like "I must get this deal" or "This deal will make me happy." If we think that one particular deal will "make us happy"—of course, we'll get scared.

Letting go of the idea "this one thing will make me happy" relates to "Rule #1: Eliminate your desires." You find new power by converting a *want* (or desire) into a *preference*. So during a pitch, you "eliminate your desires" by turning down the urgency. Instead, you tell yourself: "I *prefer* that they go for my deal. Still, it's a big universe with lots of other positive outcomes."

Let's continue with *"Rule #2: Be excellent in the presence of others."* How? Rehearse, rehearse, rehearse—and not just solo in your living room. Get trusted friends and family to be your audience. Have them toss you tough questions so you get used to answering them. With enough rehearsal, you start to feel on a visceral level that you're developing skills.

Finally, we explore *"Rule #3: Withdraw."* You do that by sitting down and being calm about silence. By that I mean, you avoid letting silence wrack you with doubt and concern. Calm yourself down by saying internally: "Silence is good. They're thinking. I *know* I did well. I like how I mentioned the funny part when Sarah confronts Joe with . . ."

Wait for the other person(s) to say something. Again, do *not* ask for validation. That shows weakness. And weakness is a threat to the reptile brain. It elicits a subconscious worry on the listener's part. Subconscious thoughts may arise: "Why is she nervous? Is there a hidden catch here?"

When you finish your presentation, many people expect you to pursue them for their response. Do not do it. Instead you "withdraw" by sitting quietly, a smile on your face. Let them come to you—that is, let them break the silence and say something.

Another Way to Deal with Fear: Use Effort–Goals and Result–Goals

An *Effort–Goal* is something in your power. For example, you control how many phone calls you make in a day. On the other hand, a *Result–Goal* depends on outside forces. You do *not* control if someone picks up the phone or if their voicemail system cuts you off in 30 seconds.

Separating things into Effort–Goals and Result–Goals brings some peace of mind. How? You get to feel proud of yourself for accomplishing your Effort–Goals.

For example, a screenwriter can actually feel better about her career. She can *control her efforts* related to part of her screenwriting career. She controls her own writing schedule. For example, I tend to write the first thing each morning. (That's how I have 20 books up on Amazon.com including *Darkest Secrets of the Film Industry Every Actor Should Know* and *Darkest Secrets of Film Directing*.)

Earlier in this book, I mentioned an empowering plan for the screenwriter: Have three screenplays:
1. One screenplay in the marketplace
2. One screenplay you are completing
3. One screenplay you are starting.

With three screenplay projects, the screenwriter can practice some nonattachment toward finding a deal for only one screenplay. So as you can see, having Effort–Goals and Result–Goals actually is part of a process of practicing nonattachment.

Producers can have Effort–Goals related to:
1. How many phone calls one makes toward securing a meeting
2. How many networking events one attends toward gaining new contacts (for opportunities to pitch).

Let's say Miranda has a Result–Goal of "sell one of my screenplays within four months." She cannot control what studio executives and producers do. But she can control how often she rehearses her pitch (an Effort–Goal). So dividing her work into Effort–Goals and Result-Goals helps her with nonattachment (that we talked about above). She *prefers* to gain the result of selling a screenplay in four months. But she does *not* demand (or stand in desperation) to sell a screenplay to a particular person she pitches to on a given day.

When you demonstrate a sense of ease that nonattachment gives you, you exude a form of power. In his compelling book *Power: Why Some People Have It—And Others Don't,* Stanford University professor Jeffrey Pfeffer emphasized the process of cognitive discounting. Pfeffer wrote: "Cognitive discounting [is the process that] once people have formed an impression of another, they disregard any information that is inconsistent with their initial ideas." You want cognitive discounting to work in your favor. How? Look into practicing nonattachment so that you give a first impression of calm confidence. Further, divide your work into Effort–Goals and Result–Goals. In fact, reward yourself for achieving your Effort–Goals. For example, give yourself a treat for rehearsing your pitch five days in a row. This process will help you enter a room with calmness instead of desperation.

The practices of nonattachment and Effort–Goals/Result–Goals will help you foster a first impression of confidence in yourself and your project. People often take another person at face value.

Points to Remember:

- **Darkest Secret #6: Show fear and you're fried.**

- **Your Countermeasure:**

Be sure to show NO behaviors asking for validation. Develop nonattachment that any particular listener must say yes during your pitch. *Avoid* showing neediness because neediness is a threat to the reptile brain—and that's the road to a "no." Instead, separate your work into Effort–Goals and Result–Goals to foster calmness.

DARKEST SECRET #7: SOME PEOPLE WILL TRY TO MAKE YOU FAIL

Researchers note that most people demonstrate a natural resistance to new ideas. And resistance in a vile form comes out as a listener trying to make you fail. They'll interrupt you, make you wait in the lobby until you feel small and powerless, or even ridicule what you're saying.

Why do people resist? Because they want to assert their autonomy. If someone's new idea pushes on their current biases or even pushes them to get out of inertia (to commit to pledge funds), people often feel threatened. Many times, you're presenting to someone who has greater wealth and higher status. How do they use that? They demonstrate their power. For example, Sarah, a producer, answers an invitation from a wealthy investor named Miranda. She arrives to find two underlings waiting for her in the conference room. But no Miranda. The underlings explain that Sarah is to explain her project to them. Sarah replies, "I've only got 20 minutes before my next appointment. I'm looking to see if you people keep appointments and are trustworthy. So find Miranda and we'll get going. Or we can forget today."

Oren Klaff talks about using a reply like Sarah's to collapse a power frame by using a time frame. As mentioned earlier, a frame is a mental structure that shapes how a person sees the world. A power frame often communicates: "I (the potential investor) have the power. You are supplicating me. I may deign to grant you a favor—if you amuse me and I have nothing better to do at the moment."

The time frame conveys that things need to get done because of deadlines and other priorities need attention.

You need to think carefully about whether you want to use a tactic of collapsing a power frame with a time frame. It's important to notice that powerful people *respect* others who respect themselves. However, if you come across as arrogant you can torpedo a business relationship before it begins. One method is to use your *tone of voice*. You could say in a light tone: "So I encourage you to find Miranda and we'll get something done. Or we can forget today."

Yes, it will take rehearsal to say this in a light manner. You want to come across as confident and calm. You'll need to have people give you feedback as to whether you can pull that off.

Here are methods you can use to deal with resistance and associated behaviors that might trip you up.

Method #1: Seize Alpha Status

We usually pitch to people with greater wealth and power than ourselves. In fact, the executive or investor feels comfortable using a power frame. The executive seeks to be the Alpha in any situation, and with the rest of the world as betas (underlings). Alphas use *beta traps,* which are patterns that get just about anyone to feel unsure or hesitant. Beta traps include making you wait or talking on the phone or interrupting you as you make a pitch.

Another tough truth is: *people resist betas.*

For example, if a politician who has flip–flopped continuously tries to quote Martin Luther King, Jr.'s "I have a dream" speech, he does *not* get traction. Why? He's a beta. Just a puppet on the strings of his ambition and what his handlers think people want to hear.

On the other hand, if one hears *Martin Luther King, Jr.* exclaim: "I have a dream that my four little children will one day live in a nation where they will not be judged by the color of their skin but by the content of their character," they feel moved by not only King's oratory skills but his authority borne of his consistent actions and who he is.

So when you pitch, seize Alpha status. What you're doing is gaining situational status. That is, you have power because you're bringing something valuable to the table. Act like you know that fact!

As I shared above, one way to seize Alpha status is to use your time frame to collapse a power frame. When Sarah said, "I've only got 20 minutes before my next appointment. I'm looking to see if you people keep appointments and are trustworthy. So find Miranda and we'll get going. Or we can forget today," she asserted a number of things:

a) She's busy and important.
b) She has the moral authority. She's on time, and she expects Miranda (and underlings) to "keep appointments and be trustworthy."

During your pitch, not only can you seize Alpha status, but you can maintain it. In fact, you have to. Not forever, of course. When you've left the room, the executive or investor continues having more wealth and power. Indeed, that is why you're talking to them. But you want them to help make a movie. So for this meeting, during this pitch, you need to become the leader.

Maintain Alpha Status by Handling Tough Questions

The best lawyers do a process of preparing the opposing side's case. The idea is to figure out ahead of time what their opponent will do. Similarly, I have my clients and my graduate students prepare *10 Worst Questions You Do Not Want to Answer*. I encourage you do the same as part of your preparation of your pitch. Also, prepare two answers per question.

Here are examples of "Worst Questions":
1. Have you ever produced a movie before?
2. How much money did your last film make?
3. What makes you think you can direct a feature film when you've only directed music videos?

You need to rehearse ways to respond to tough questions so that you feel prepared. For more about how to "catch a tough question," see the later section of this book entitled: *Book Five: How to Answer Tough Questions.*

Method #2: Design and Deliver Your Pitch to Create Hot Cognitions

Earlier in this book, I talked of a *hot cognition* as liking something before you know much about it. I also mentioned how you can develop "wanting" in your listener. Avoid getting bogged down in talking about financials. Get the listener on your side by intriguing them (the intrigue frame) and "prizing." Prizing means: you and your project are the prize. Demonstrate how attractive your project is, how exciting, how profitable, how intriguing.

Method #3: Use Time to Strengthen Your Pitch

Researchers note that human beings' attention span falls apart at 20 minutes. So design your pitch to come in at 20 minutes (or less). You'll also gain Alpha status by emphasizing to a private investor: "I only have 20 minutes to describe this opportunity. And then we'll have some time to talk."

One great detail is that your listener will be *relieved* that this is *not* going to be a drawn out hour and a half presentation. How does this relate to people trying to trip you up? If the investor knows that your pitch will take 20 minutes, she's likely to let you go ahead instead of trying to cut you off with disruptive questions to get to the heart of the matter. Presumably, in only 20 minutes, you're forced to design your pitch as focused and concise.

Method #4: "Dole Out Some Alpha Status"

During your pitch, you've seized Alpha status, and Oren Klaff recommends "doling out some Alpha status." You do that by praising someone in the room for a comment that supports your points.

You can do that with phrases:

- Good point, Sarah. That leads us to the next part I'm talking about.
- Yes, Mark. That's an essential part of this opportunity.
- Excellent, Valerie. That *is* the hot button for our target market.

Dole out Alpha Status to get people on your side. Dr. Michael V. Pantalon in his book, *Instant Influence: How to Get Anyone to Do Anything—Fast,* wrote: "People take action when they hear themselves say *why* they want to." Why is this important? When you praise someone in the Dole Out Alpha Status pattern, you're reinforcing that person's reason to say "yes" to your film project.

Method #5: Neutralize Resistance By Using Memes

Richard Brodie, author of *Virus of the Mind,* writes about the *meme,* which is any information that gets replicated. Why is this important? When you're pitching, you want your idea, that the investor's best action is to invest in your film, *to be replicated.*

So it helps to understand what is the nature of an idea that has "graduated" to the level of a meme.

Some researchers call a meme an "idea virus." Brodie describes six forms of meme. Other people use different lists but I like his. So here they are, complete with my own comments.

1. Elitism

People like to feel special. Smarter than others. More attractive. Taller, faster, funnier, better with money, more perceptive—you name it. In recent years, studio executives have been scrambling for "the next *Harry Potter* franchise." A number of projects have been greenlit (approved) including *The Golden Compass* (which stumbled) and *Percy Jackson & the Olympians: The Lightning* Thief (which gained a sequel).

If someone is pitching the next *Harry Potter* franchise, she wants the studio executive to feel like he will be someone who "discovered" the next mega–franchise. Imagine the prestige, the power, the opportunities that come with that! And the studio executive will froth at the mouth to join the *elite* of the industry.

2. Evangelism

Many independent films end up financed by private investors who believed and wanted the word spread. So advice to a producer of an independent film is: "Find your people." This reminds me of the time I interviewed Carly Fiorina, former CEO of Hewlett-Packard. She said, "Find people who believe as you do. They're out there."

The *Merriam–Webster Dictionary* includes the words "militant or crusading zeal" in a definition of *evangelism*. So see if your film is somehow a "positive crusade." Find people who want to join your movement.

3. Low risk, high reward

Many films are designed to have a modest budget, making higher returns possible. A filmmaker may say, "Our comedy is directed toward African Americans. You probably know that Tyler Perry's film *Diary of a Mad Black Woman* was made for $5.5 million and earned over $50 million. Our film is budgeted at $2 million. We'll make that back with just DVD, Blu-ray, TV and ancillary markets."

4. Tradition

Appealing to tradition related to filmmaking can be tricky. Here's a possible approach. Producer Sarah says, "The reason I'm here is because Universal is sharp and dedicated to quality filmmaking. Look, you guys released A *Beautiful Mind* . . ." She's implying that Universal has a tradition of releasing prestige films in addition to their other material.

5. Fear of punishment

Producer Sarah says, "You know you don't want to be known as the one who passed on *She Knows More* with [name director], [name actor] and an Oscar-winning screenwriter." Sarah implies that the studio executive will look bad to people in the industry and may suffer when trying to find work at another studio.

6. Crisis

Want someone's attention? Get them to believe that we're living in a time of crisis. Or that a crisis is imminent. Crisis is the center of broadcast news programs. It harks back to the journalism motto: "If it bleeds, it leads."

Crisis is also the center of dramatic structure. For example, you will probably structure how you describe your film around a crisis in the main character's life. Max Adams, screenwriter and author, developed a formula that helps you clearly explain almost any film:

(Title) is a (genre) about (protagonist) who must (objective) or else (dire consequences if protagonist fails).

Her example was for Ron Howard's film *Apollo 13*:

Apollo 13 *is a drama about three astronauts who must repair their spacecraft or they will suffocate in space before reaching home.*

A number of agents like to create a "crisis" so that studio executives scramble for a screenplay. In essence, the agent starts a bidding war. They invent a deadline. Some studio executives will do a pre-emptive strike and offer $1 million or more for a screenplay (even from a first–time screenwriter) to outdo their competitors.

So what does all of the above information about memes relate to how some people will try to make you fail? If you're smart and do your homework, you'll design your pitch around memes and you make your pitch like "brain candy." And this reduces resistance!

A Final Word about Resistance:
Studio executives often push you and test you in a meeting to see if they want to have you anywhere near them. Linda Obst, producer of *Contact* (starring Jodie Foster and Matthew McConaughey) and *Sleepless in Seattle* (starring Tom Hanks and Meg Ryan) told me, "Be someone they want to have around." By that she meant you need to develop rapport. She learned the hard way; she had been dropped from the film *Flashdance* even though she had originated the project.

So it's a delicate balance. You need to demonstrate your expertise and confidence in yourself. However, you must avoid coming across as self-absorbed and arrogant. Not everyone will like you. But it's important that you respect yourself and give off that energy. And gain people's respect.

Expect resistance to your pitch. Prepare. Rehearse how you'll use one or many of the above methods.

Points to Remember:

- **Darkest Secret #7: Some people will try to make you fail.**
- **Your Countermeasure:**

Prepare to receive resistance. Develop and deliver your pitch to inspire a hot cognition. Learn to gain Alpha status during your pitch. And also, make space for your listener to feel autonomy. When they feel safe, they're less likely to offer disruptive resistance. Consider using the six forms of a meme: Elitism, Evangelism, Low Risk–High Reward, Tradition, Fear of Punishment, and Crisis.

BOOK 2

This section is based on my presentation entitled: "Tom Marcoux on Pitching Secrets for Your Success."

Here we talk about how you can create a relationship with investors so that they'll want to invest in the project that you're offering. We need to connect with investors even before they sit down to the table. And we need to become liked by them.

PART 1: HOW TO MEET AND ENGAGE INVESTORS WHO MAY BE RECEPTIVE TO YOUR PITCH

1. How do you become liked?

To become liked, be sure to listen at the beginning of your first interaction. Avoid presenting to them right from the beginning. Instead, start by trying to get to know them.

For example, before a presentation, I was in the restroom, brushing my teeth. An investor walked up to the nearby sink and said, "You're making every detail work well."

"Yes," I replied with a smile. With this conversation, I started building a rapport. Between pitching sessions, I talked with this investor outside of the presentation room. I asked questions, and he told me about Hawaii and his trips and about some special business opportunities. I knew he was sharing parts of his life with me because I was listening to him.

The way to become liked is to become a good listener. To do that, you need to ask gentle, comfortable questions.

Here are examples:

- "So what brings you to this presentation?"
- "Who do you know here?"

- "Have you met Mark, our host?"
- "How did you come to know Mark?"

2. How do you make people feel comfortable?
Move like you're confident. This is important because we often feel uncomfortable when we're around someone who fidgets or seems jittery. Some people look like they're "scrunched down" as if they're trying to take up the least amount of space. They hunch over with their back. Over 25 years ago, I felt shy, and I sought training in how to move as a confident person. I learned to have my diaphragm up and away from my belly button. This makes me stand taller. Research shows that people who stand tall, with good posture and poise, look confident.

If you act in a way that is confident, people are comfortable around you. They're *not* comfortable with someone who looks socially awkward. They feel uncomfortable around those who seem nervous or upset.

Even if you don't feel confident, you can act in a manner that appears confident. One of my clients from several years ago would imagine himself as Sean Connery as James Bond. He would walk like Sean Connery. And in that way, my client would move with confidence.

You need to model the behavior of confident people—observe them and then move like them. Decide for yourself: "How would I move if I were confident?" When you move like a confident person often enough, you will start *to feel like* a confident person because when you change your posture, you actually feel different.

This focus on moving like a confident person relates to how you interact with an investor (or studio executive or producer) before you sit down and make a pitch.

When I train people in a workshop, I have them do "group work." They practice their "confident walk-up," and they practice listening. The idea is, at a networking event, you walk up to a group in a direct way. You hold your glass of water (yes, water, so that you don't accidentally spill something that may stain clothing) and you listen to whoever is speaking. You nod and smile. You introduce yourself when there is a lull in the conversation.

So what does all of the above information about memes relate to how some people will try to make you fail? If you're smart and do your homework, you'll design your pitch around memes and you make your pitch like "brain candy." And this reduces resistance!

PART 2: LEARN SECRETS OF A SCIENCE–BASED APPROACH TO CREATE INSTANT RAPPPORT

Some people say that they're not good at small talk. The truth is: small talk is just about connecting. To initiate or participate in small talk, you can ask things like:

- "So what are your hobbies?"
- "What are you looking forward to?"

These gentle questions help you connect with someone on a personal level. I've raised money for a number of projects, and every single time the person invested in me as a person—not just the project.

Unfortunately, many of us forget about personally connecting with the investor. We get caught up with "just making the presentation perfect" as if the presentation itself will make people want to invest. No. They're not just investing in a project; they are mostly investing in you. In fact, after Steve Jobs was ousted from Apple, he had a meeting with Ross Perot. Perot immediately placed $8 million into Jobs' new company called NeXT. Perot's comment was basically that he invests in extraordinary people. It's likely that Perot made a lot of money because Jobs required

Apple to buy his company NeXT as one of the conditions of Jobs' return to Apple.

Perot invested in Jobs, the person. That's why you need to connect with people in a "person to person" way right from the start.

A science–based approach to creating rapport is built, in part, on insights found in neuro–linguistic programming. People connect with people based on how they sound, how fast they talk, and how loud they are:

a. How do you sound? (tonality)
b. How fast do you talk? (pace)
c. How loud are you? (volume)

If you're talking with someone who talks quietly, then you talk quietly. If you're talking with someone from a Southern state of the U.S. who talks slowly, then you talk slowly (as compared to a New Yorker). If you're talking with someone who has an intensity in their tone, then you take on an "intensity" as well.

Tonality, pace, and volume are important elements for you to use to create instant rapport with someone. Researchers note that people can like someone based on whether there's a match in tonality, pace, and volume. Practitioners of neuro–linguistic programming call this process "mirroring and matching."

What it comes down to is this: *People tend to like others who seem similar to them.* So you want to appear similar to the person you are trying to influence. This includes body language. When people are in rapport, they sit in a similar way. They may sit with one knee over the other, but they have the opposite knee on top. It looks like they are a mirror image of each other. You see this with business partners and even romantic partners. They look similar in body position.

The mirroring of body position is a technique someone tried to use on me once; unfortunately, she wasn't subtle in her approach. She had probably taken a course and was clearly matching the position of my arms. However, she didn't wait 30 seconds before attempting to mirror my actions. Whenever I happened to fold my arms, she would fold her arms a couple of seconds later. Too obvious. I caught her. I didn't say anything to her; I just filed this detail away mentally. She may have simply been trying to connect with me, or she may have been trying to manipulate me. Either way, I did not know what her intentions were, and she lost her chance at creating rapport with me by being too obvious.

To appropriately mirror and match someone, you should instead wait 30-40 seconds before you shift your own body position. Otherwise, you'll be caught. An old phrase holds: A technique known is a technique blown. You want to be subtle.

Another way to create instant rapport is to look for clues about how an investor likes to take in input:

- *How does the investor like to receive input?*

The three modes of receiving input are visual, auditory, and kinesthetic.

Visual:
Some investors prefer to see a video as part of your presentation.

Auditory:
Some investors want to hear testimonials—perhaps to have a conversation with someone who has invested with you before.

Kinesthetic:
Some investors have a "touch" or "feeling in my own body" approach. For example, if a presenter tells them that a deal will save them money, they prefer to use a calculator and punch in the numbers and prove the savings to themselves.

The question becomes, "How do we find out what a person prefers?" If you hear that someone has purchased a car (or house) recently, you could ask something like: "Oh, how did you know that the car was the right one for you?"

Then you listen closely:

- "I saw myself sitting in the car, reflected on the showroom's window." (visual)
- "My spouse told me what she found valuable about the car." (auditory)
- "I felt the power of the engine." (kinesthetic)

Once you have some clues as to what the investor prefers as his mode of receiving input, then gear your presentation to emphasize that particular mode (visual, auditory, or kinesthetic).

Listening can give you clues about how an investor likes to receive information.
Pay close attention to investors' offhand comments to each other as well. You may happen to overhear investors talking, and one says, "I have all this email. I hate email. Why can't they pick up the phone and call me, and give me the facts in two minutes? I don't want to read a long report in an email." When you hear someone say he'd like to receive a phone call, you can surmise that he is an "auditory person."

If another investor says, "Just send me a link. I'd like to see the webpage," then you know that this person prefers input in the visual mode.

If you're talking about ROI (return on investment) and the investor pulls out her calculator, then you have a good idea that this person is "kinesthetic." She needs to touch the calculator and work the ideas through with her hands. Just telling her something does *not* seize her attention. Instead, she needs to work it through for herself.

Pay close attention to investors' offhand comments to each other.

PART 3: OVERCOME THE "6 RAPPORT–BREAKERS" AND GET THE AUDIENCE ON YOUR SIDE

When you are going to do a presentation, make sure you get to the site early so that you can talk with the investors one–to–one. Connect with them as one person to another. Make sure that you mingle. To mingle successfully, you need to avoid the following 6 Rapport-Breakers (which I have formed as questions):

1. Are you talking too much about yourself?
2. Are you using a fake smile?
3. Are you "hesitating"?
4. Do you lack energy?
5. Are you complaining or telling "poor me" stories?
6. Have you dressed effectively?

Let's look at each of these in more detail.

1. Are you talking too much about yourself?
Do *not* approach your pitching situation as "Oh, no! The clock is ticking. I've got to tell them my resume. I've got to hit them more

than once with my pitch!" Instead, realize that you're establishing rapport when you're listening. They like you when you listen, and when they like you, they'll be more likely to listen to you when it's your turn to do the talking.

You may even want to do some listening while you're making your presentation. We'll talk more about that later in this book.

The way to avoid talking too much about yourself is to ask a question (after you've talked for 20 seconds). In other words, you want to get the other person talking about herself. Avoid hitting the person with your resume right off the bat or hitting her so hard with your pitch that she falls over.

2. *Are you using a fake smile?*
Avoid having a "pasted on" smile. I was trained in the Dale Carnegie method, which emphasizes the need to smile. But it's got to be a genuine smile—a smile that naturally comes up and then naturally drops from your face.

Some people smile too much. They may feel vulnerable, or they may try too hard to be ingratiating. It becomes too much.

Instead, leaders who are confident smile when it's appropriate. And then the smile goes away.

When you meet someone, focus on appropriate thoughts. That's how you get a genuine smile to light up your own face. Good thoughts include:
- I'm glad that I'm meeting you.
- We're going to connect.
- This is going to be a terrific interaction.
- You might become a friend of mine.
- I can help you. I'm going to find out how I can be of service to you.

The above thoughts will generate a genuine smile.

As a film director and trained actor, I know that actors can put genuine emotion on their faces if they have the right focus. They also use an "objective." An objective is a tool for the actors to get absolutely clear about what they want–that is, what they will gain or achieve.

Here's a possible "objective" you can adopt:

- I'm going to make this potential investor like me (and I'll know that they like me because they'll smile in return).

When I have an "objective," everything will flow with it. How will I get them to like me? By making it very easy for them to talk with me. I'm going to get them to feel good as I'm listening to them. It's easy for them to feel good because they'll know I value their intelligence, their insight, and their kindness. I'm going to let them know this with my demeanor. And because I'm focused in this way, I can approach them with a genuine smile–not a fake smile.

3. Are you "hesitating"?
This takes us back to "move with confidence." People who are confident take up space. They do *not* have their bodies clenched together with their arms folded. Instead, they take up space and gesture widely with their hands. Males tend to stand with their feet shoulder–width apart. Some female executives prefer to stand with one foot forward and not with their feet apart in a "linebacker" stance.

Leaders, male and female, stand with good posture, with the chest away from the belly. You need to do the same.

4. Do you lack energy?
Whatever you do, don't give off a "low energy" vibe. No one invests when the person does not show the strength, energy, and enthusiasm to get the job done.

For example, I once sat in a room with investors listening to an older man presenting. His material was great. But he was also quite sick—perhaps with a cold or the flu. I had a fleeting thought during his presentation: "This guy has 20–30 years of experience, but I don't know if he's going to survive the evening!" We in the audience honestly didn't know if the guy would prove strong enough to get the film project done.

You need to show that you have energy, confidence, and strength because every project needs a strong, consistent, and persistent leader.

5. Are you complaining or telling "poor me" stories?
Do *not* walk into the room complaining about the traffic. Don't complain about anything, in fact. Certainly, do not complain about previous investors on other projects! And definitely avoid "poor me" stories.

For example, let's say you have a broken leg. Don't say anything like this: "Oh, I broke my leg, and it hurt so bad. I was in the hospital for 10 days and..." No one wants to hear any of that. That kind of talk breaks rapport. We all have our own pain; we don't want someone else's pain, too. Instead, say something brief but positive, such as "Oh, yeah, I broke it skiing, but I can't wait to get on the slopes again."

6. Have you dressed effectively?
As author Roger Mellot said, "It would be [ineffective] for someone to wear a tuxedo and sell tractor equipment." In Hollywood, people tend to avoid ties. Perhaps some of the executives (known as "the suits") wear ties. But the creative people tend to avoid ties. One of my mentors, years ago, said, "To dress effectively, you need to dress for the job you want. Maybe not the job you have." To create rapport, it is okay to dress a little "above" what the other people are wearing, yet you do not want to dress "below" what they're wearing.

In meeting many people, I've noticed that the wealthy tend to dress comfortably. But to get them to invest in your project, you need to dress well. Your chosen style may vary depending on your audience. Dress like their advisors—someone they take seriously. Avoid coming in with ragged jeans, proclaiming,

"I'm an artiste!" The investors want you to be a business-person—someone they can trust with their money.

(It's all about trust. In fact, I wrote a book, along these lines, entitled *Be Heard and Be Trusted*.)

PART 4: AVOID "DON'TS OF FIRST IMPRESSIONS" AND USE "GREAT FIRST—IMPRESSION CREATORS"

Here are the "Don'ts" of making a first impression:

1. Don't give too much information.
2. Don't miss the investor's "preferred order."
3. Don't rush, which can make the investor feel agitated.

As I discuss each "Don't," I'll include the "Great First-Impression Creator" you can use as a replacement.

1. Don't give too much information
People tune out after too many details. *Instead,* make a good impression by providing the most significant details. Ask questions to find out what the investor wants to "drill down" about. To drill down is to go deeper in one particular area of the subject.

2. Don't miss the investor's "preferred order"
Listen very carefully. The investor will tell you what he or she is interested in. If the investor wants to hear about ROI (return on investment) first, you'll know—when you listen carefully.

For example, you can be in a conversation with a potential investor who says, "One of my favorite investments was The Acme Project." You ask, "What about the Acme Project attracted you? What was important for you to know that helped you make that decision to go with the Acme Project?"

Then the investor replies, "First, I wanted to know about the ROI. Next, I wanted to know if it was 'first in—first out'."

"First in—first out" means that the initial investors put their money in first and get their money back first—before producers and actors get their money (participation in profits). Investors like "first in—first out." You need to realize, too, that venture capitalists generally aren't concerned about the actual company they're investing in; they don't care if it gets sold or gets cut into little pieces. What they are focused on is doubling (or quadrupling) their money in five years. So you need to be extremely careful when getting venture capital, if you're thinking of going in that direction, because venture capitalists often are only interested in making money—not in the "cause" or the uplifting product or "making a great company."

So in essence, you need to use this Great First-Impression Creator: Listen carefully about the investor's preferred order of receiving information so that you can tailor your talk accordingly.

3. Don't rush, which can make the investor feel agitated

Remember that when you meet with the investor before you give the presentation, your primary job is to *connect* as well as to respond to the questions or ideas that the investor brings up. Avoid trying to give your whole presentation in that first conversation. If you try to get "all" of the information in, you'll probably rush. When you rush, the investor may miss details and feel frustrated. Further, you'll feel uncomfortable and that discomfort transfers to the investor. Along these lines, researchers speak of mirror-neurons (brain cells) that get human beings feeling similar things.

Remember, too, that when you make a presentation, that is only the beginning of the business relationship with the potential investor. When I've gained funds by enlisting investors, I've noticed it is truly a relationship of trust that I was building. So don't rush; don't make the investor uncomfortable. Don't overdo it in the first meeting.

So in essence, you need to use this *Great First–Impression Creator:* Slow down and make sure that you are connecting with the person in a first conversation.

In summary, here are the three *Great First–Impression Creators*:

1. Provide the most significant details (after you ask questions).
2. Listen and discover the investor's "preferred order."
3. Slow down and make sure that you are *connecting* with the person in a first conversation.

PART 5: ELIMINATE "TERRIBLE SHOW-STOPPERS" AND REPLACE THEM WITH RAPPORT-CREATORS

The phrase "Terrible Show-Stoppers" rose in my thoughts when I was in a particular investor meeting. Two producers offered a deal that stunned me. It led to my first "Terrible Show-Stopper" below:

1. Don't offer a deal that "offends" the investor

How could a deal offend the investor? Listen to this so–called deal (I'll change the numbers to give the two producers privacy). "We're looking for $7 million. We'll put $1 million toward the movie. And $6 million will go to us. Then we'll be done with the project." What? The producers are going to get off the train before the project is even done? They're not going to ride the train with the risk–with the investors? They're going to get $6 million in their pocket, but they're only going to put $1 million in the movie? What is that?! It is simply offensive to the potential investor to offer a deal such as that.

Let's take a moment to notice:

a) Investors like it when you share the risk.
b) Investors like it when the majority of the funds go to making the film project high quality.
c) Investors like it when the producers get "rewarded" only when the film makes money.

2. Don't "instruct" the investor

Some of us make the mistake of "going into presentation mode" as if we're a teacher who is going to teach the investors about Hollywood. We're going to "teach them" about the structure of this investment. We'll "teach them" about how we're so smart and know what we're doing. If you do this, you'll ignite all of the negative emotions that people felt when they were growing up and had a lousy teacher or two. Lousy teachers talked "at" them and not "with" them.

Instead, adopt the attitude of *sharing* the investment opportunity with the potential investor.

One thing I do is bring a bar stool so that I can sit down during a significant portion of my presentations. This changes my energy. I am talking with people instead of merely giving a performance. Talk with your audience of investors in the manner of a series of one–to–one conversations. Give a paragraph to one person before you move on to talking with the next section of the audience.

Consider using a bar stool and sitting down. Don't instruct the investors; don't lecture them. Talk with the investors. Realize that you're creating relationships from scratch.

3. Don't display "ego"—doing so suggests that you won't listen to the investor's ideas

Avoid displaying your "ego." I understand you're an expert at what you do. Perhaps you've been in the film industry for fifteen years. You know what you're doing. You know how to work with a focus group. You know how to re–edit a scene to get the laughter. You're an expert. We get it. The investors probably saw your biography before they entered the room. You don't have to be a know–it–all. You do need to know your stuff, but you also need to listen to your investors.

The investors that I've met have been very intelligent people. They know what they know. They're "live wires"; they pay attention. They're on top of certain blogs and reading *The Wall Street Journal.* I've been in meetings in which the conversations were golden—that is, I was learning a lot at the time.

So when an investor offers you some ideas, take out your pen and write them down. If you can, say sincerely, "That's interesting. I'm going to give that a lot of thought. Let me take a note about that. And your name is?" Then you can say, "Well, Jacob, after my presentation, maybe we can talk more about that during the break." Or you can say, "I'm glad you brought that up. It would be good to explore that further with you."

Don't display ego. Instead, create connection.

The solutions I have shared above with you, I call Rapport–Creators.

PART 6: DEVELOP THE "ELEVATOR SPEECH" (OR ELEVATOR PITCH) FOR YOU & YOUR FILM

The "Elevator Speech" or "Elevator Pitch" is about 20 seconds in which you vividly express the essence of something. You need one for yourself, and you need one for your film.

I have two different Elevator Speeches because I'm both a member of the film industry and I'm a professional speaker.

Here are a couple of examples:

"Hi, I'm Tom Marcoux. I'm a producer, director, and writer. Currently, my company has three franchises: *TimePulse* (that's science fiction), *Jack AngelSword* (that's fantasy–thriller) and *Crystal Pegasus* (that's a children's book and a trilogy of animated feature films). I won a special award at the Emmys. And a previous feature film I directed was taken by the distributor to the Cannes Film market."

Here's one for me as a speaker:

"Hi, I'm Tom Marcoux. I'm known as America's Communication

Coach. Have you ever felt you could rise to the next level but you had some obstacles in your way? Well, what I do is help people like you use Time Leverage—to get more done and feel better doing it. I do that as a personal coach, speech coach, speaker, and author with 20 books on Amazon.com."

So you need an Elevator Speech for yourself and one for your film, too.

Here's a pitch for one of my films, *2 Days to Hollywood.*

"2 *Days to Hollywood* is a comedy with ghosts. Two friends are on a road trip to Hollywood. The young guy, about 20, is typing on his laptop to finish a screenplay before they arrive in Hollywood. If he wins a screenplay contest, he'll get to direct his first movie. The older guy has had his heart stopped, and since that time he can see ghosts. And there's an evil ghost that will doing anything to stop them. *Anything*."

All of the above pitches to me are "works-in-progress"—I keep refining them and adapting them to situations that come up.

Good Elevator Speeches have two elements:

1. They seize the listener's attention.
2. They finish well—often with suspense.

1. Good elevator speeches seize the listener's attention

For this aspect, I use what I like to call the "The 'You' Question + My Answer + Desired Result" pattern. Let's look back at my sample elevator speech for my role as a speaker.

After introducing myself, I went right into a "you" question–a question designed to make the listener answer "yes," even if only rhetorically. I asked, "Have you ever felt you could rise to the next level but you had some obstacles in your way?" First of all, notice that I used "you," which naturally makes a listener perk up ("Hey, he's talkin' to me!").

Second, I used a kind of question that will make just about anyone nod in affirmation ("Yeah, I've felt like that before...").

After asking the "you" question, I supplied an answer to that question—or more specifically, I supplied a solution to the common problem raised in the question. In my speech, I said, "Well, what I do is help people like you use Time Leverage..." I also threw in some ways in which I could assist the listener with that: "...I do that as a personal coach, speech coach, speaker, and author with 20 books on Amazon.com."

Finally, I pointed out the desired result—what the listener can gain by using my solution or by taking advantage of my services. In my speech, I told the listener that my assistance could help him "get more done and feel better doing it." Now...how can anybody say "no" to that?

2. Good elevator speeches finish well

For this component, I like to use the "Imagine to Suspense" technique. For example, you'll notice in my pitch about *2 Days to Hollywood* that I did *not* tell how the story ends. I said, "And there's an evil ghost that will do anything to stop them. Anything." You need to make your listener imagine the possibilities and then leave her in suspense. Why? Because you want her to take the next step—to read your screenplay or to consider your marketing plan.

When I talk about the "Imagine to Suspense" pattern, I am pointing to the process of getting the investors to go with you. If you get them imagining, then you've captured their attention, and you've drawn them into the story.

PART 7: CRAFT AN ATTENTION–GRABBING "LOGLINE" FOR YOUR SCREENPLAY

What's a logline? It's a tool used by the film industry to quickly tell what a movie is about so that a studio executive or producer can decide if he or she wants to hear more.

Here are examples:

"A 17th century tale of adventure on the Caribbean Sea where the roguish yet charming Captain Jack Sparrow joins forces with a young blacksmith in a gallant attempt to rescue the Governor of England's daughter and reclaim his ship."—logline for *Pirates of the Caribbean*

"After being falsely convicted of the murder of his wife, a once prominent surgeon escapes custody to find the real killer and clear his name."—logline for *The Fugitive*

To be attention–grabbing, a logline needs to have three key elements working together: a relatable hero with a big want and a big obstacle. Let's examine the *rough draft* of a sample logline and see how it incorporates these key elements:

Susan is a caring, grammar school teacher who ends up with a flash drive of material impacting national security. Chased by enemy agents, she wants to protect her son, survive, and get the flash drive to General Hatley, her ex-husband's father.

1. *Relatable Hero*: "Susan is a caring, grammar school teacher. . ." Many of us can remember one truly good teacher, so Susan is a character that we can connect to or relate to. And what makes this movie's idea even more compelling is the fact that our relatable hero is facing an unusual problem—something out of the ordinary.

2. *Big Want:* ". . .protect her son, survive, and get the flash drive to General Hatley, her ex-husband's father."
Once Susan is placed in this unusual situation, she has a powerful set of motivations–not only for herself and her son to survive but also for national security to be protected.

3. *Big Obstacle:* "Chased by enemy agents. . ."
Now...it wouldn't be fun if Susan didn't have to work to get those wants of hers, so she needs to have something big in her way.

Loglines require that you perform many rewrites to pare down the words to the most compelling set. The above sample is nowhere near its final form, but it's a good start because it does contain those key elements that will garner it the attention it deserves.

* * *

The above First Seven Parts form, in my workshops, the session "Connect."Now, we move onto the next session, "Gain Trust," with Part Eight . . .

PART 8: PROVIDE THE RIGHT FACTS & STATS TO SHOW YOU KNOW WHAT YOU'RE TALKING ABOUT

I was in an audience of investors while observing a number of filmmakers give their pitches. One filmmaker went on and on about a number of music artists. I watched the faces of the investors, and I saw that they did not know who these music artists were. Nor did they care. Yet the filmmaker continued to go on and on about them. The music artists were, in fact, relevant to his project, but he hadn't made the connection clear.

This example illustrates an important principle: As you present, watch the faces of the investors, and adjust your approach accordingly.

This leads to my first question about your pitch:

1. Can you simplify it?
In the situation of the filmmaker talking about the music artists, he should have immediately made their relevance clear by saying something like, "These six artists' albums went platinum."

The idea is to share the right facts and statistics, and if you can simplify the information, all the better. That way, the investor can say, "I get it. That's all I need. I understand." The investor then can read your materials for more information if he or she wants to.

Another way to help the investors make a connection to your film idea is to compare it to well–performing films that have come before it, which leads to my next question about your pitch:

2. What are some well–chosen "Example–Films"?
Investors want to know where your film fits into the great scheme of things. How is your movie like other movies that have done well? How is it unlike the other movies, and will its unlikeness be a good thing or a bad thing? In other words, will your movie's unique twist make it more or less attractive to the movie–going audience? Here's a way you can provide this sort of information.

You can say something like, "We've looked at the marketplace. In terms of films that have the same genre as our film, we have examples at three levels. These are Good Returns; these are Excellent Returns; and these are *Great* Returns. Our movie's like this one. . ."

That is how you identify the good statistics that your investors would like to see.

But be careful in choosing your example films. You don't want to use an example that's been touted so often that it's cliché. You also don't want to use an example film whose situation was an unrepeatable anomaly.

For instance, *The Blair Witch Project* was made for $60,000 and earned over $140.5 million. You may recall that, at the time of the movie's distribution, the Internet was still in its adolescence; movies didn't get the pervasive multi-media coverage that today's movies do. The marketers for Blair Witch used a highly effective web campaign, promoting the idea that the characters were real people and that the movie itself was recovered footage. The subsequent buzz skyrocketed the movie to the top of the earnings chart. Now that the Internet has matured, however, the kind of attention that *Blair Witch* garnered via its web promotion twist can never be repeated in quite the same way, as was discovered with the recent film *Apollo 18* (another so-called "found footage" gene movie that cost approximately $5 million to make but earned only $17.6 million domestically—a respectable take but not a phenomenal one).

My point is...show your potential investors how your movie will both fit into and stand out in the marketplace, but choose wisely when selecting example films for comparison. You definitely don't want give your investors a sense of "been there, done that," nor do you wish to scare your investors with a movie that seems "too different" to be marketable.

Small films often must rely on free publicity. Back in 1987, *Hollywood Shuffle* (budget $100,000 and U.S. domestic earnings of $5.2 million) was promoted as "a movie made with credit cards." Another film, *The Ticket Outta Here* (1990) gained some publicity as being the first feature film made on Hi8 video. These details are now "been there, done that."

What really counts? That your film has something that seizes people's attention and emotions. Filmmakers often express their concerns about doing a film that is "fresh and original." Along those lines, I remember Julia Cameron's (author of *The Artist's Way*) comment: "Original means *you* are the origin of the work." Write something that moves you. That's where compelling films begin.

Sometimes investors really pay attention to whether a film has a recognizable star. For example, twin brothers–actors–filmmakers Logan and Noah Miller made their first film *Touching Home* based on their father. The genuine feelings and thoughts in the screenplay attracted actor Ed Harris to play their father.

Finally, don't make unrealistic comparisons to other films and the amounts they earned. Don't give your investors some "pie-in-the-sky fantasy" pitch. Be credible.

PART 9: CAREFULLY LISTEN TO & INCORPORATE INVESTORS' IDEAS, COMMENTS & SUGGESTIONS

Take care to have notes when you present. I guide both my clients and my graduate students (in public speaking class) to have 3 x 5 cards connected by a metal ring. If they drop the cards, the cards stay in order. When you practice a number of times, you'll find that you will not need to look down at the cards because you'll already know what's on most, if not all, of the cards. The cards are only used for backup purposes.

You know what you'll present, but you need to make space in the presentation for investors to share ideas, comments, and suggestions. Part of that space–making process is to learn your investors' names and show your appreciation for their comments.

1. How will you remember your investors' names?
Here are four steps to help you remember names:
a) Be sure that you *heard* the name. Repeat it back to the person.
b) Repeat the name in your mind while you look at the person's face.

c) Draw a grid of the table and place people's names in the grid so that you can glance at the grid. so that you can glance at the grid.
d) If someone has an unusual name, ask how to spell it. Visualize how to spell the name as you look at the person.

When someone offers an idea, you can say, "That's a terrific idea. And you are?" Then you repeat the name with something like: "Well, thank you, Steve."

Then reinforce the name, glance at your names–grid, and say something like: "I'm glad that Steve brought up that this type of film has seen good success with this demographic."

Learning names will help you make a personal connection. But it's not easy. It takes effort.

Some people say that they are not good with remembering names. I invite you to go beyond that limiting thought. Author Randy Gage wrote: "I will do what others will not do, so in the future I *can* do what others cannot do." People who practice the methods of remembering names become better at making good connections with people.

For example, I was in a situation in which remembering a person's name "Joy" was a good idea. So I thought of her boyfriend "George." And I told myself "George *enjoys* being with Joy." This mnemonic device helped me memorize Joy's name.

2. How can you express appreciation for your investors' comments? An important part of "Carefully Listen to & Incorporate Investors' Ideas, Comments & Suggestions" is to express appreciation.

Rehearse phrases like these:

- "Steve, thanks for bringing that point up. I really appreciate that."
- "George, I'm glad that you mentioned that. I'm going to give that a lot of thought."

- "Thanks, Sarah. This is terrific. Your point leads us right into this next section that I was going to talk about."

You need to practice a number of phrases that you can express sincerely. If you repeat one phrase over and over (like "Thank you for bringing that up" or "That's a good question") then you'll come across as a phony. Instead, you need to practice various ways to express appreciation.

You need to practice expressing appreciation before you give a presentation. Why? When people are in a stressful situation, they tend to fall back into their early training and their "default behaviors." Such training is often *not* helpful.

If a person got scared having to write on the blackboard in class, he or she would fall back to such fear. How do we deal with such fear? Rehearse, rehearse, rehearse. I guide my clients and graduate students to rehearse any time they feel a bit of fear. How? You can call your own answer machine (or system) and leave a message in which you practice the opening of your presentation. You can also practice two minute segments of your pitch by calling various friends and saying something like, "Is this a good time to talk?... Can I practice the two–minute closing of my pitch with you?" In essence, we need to practice new behaviors and develop new perceptions.

By the way, for many of us, it's a great idea to get a speech coach, even for just an hour or two. It's worth investing in yourself and your project to get such a coach. My clients tell me that even one hour makes a big difference in their confidence and ease in speaking.

PART 10: LEARN TO EFFECTIVELY USE THE "POWER–THREE" LISTENING METHODS

When focusing on listening, consider these three questions:

1. Is your body aligned and "listening"?
When an investor asks you a question while you're presenting, turn your whole body to face that investor. With my graduate students, I emphasize "heart faces heart."

Avoid facing sideways and looking over your shoulder. In that position it looks like the person is an afterthought to you. It looks like you really don't care. Turn your whole body toward the person, and take a step toward them—but not too close. You can even lean forward a bit. You're showing interest, but you need to avoid making the error of looking like you're intimidating anyone. People have different requirements for personal space. Say something like: "George, thanks for mentioning that. About that detail, I can say . . ."

Make sure that your body is aligned and it "appears like you're listening." Your body position can actually help you listen.

2. How can you avoid judging, defending, and the "me too—one up" trap?
These three elements (judging, defending, and the "me, too—one up" trap) fill up the space and prevent you from listening.

The first element that can disrupt the listening process is judging.

For example, an investor made his money in technology, but you have an instant judgment that the guy has no knowledge of the film industry. Avoid saying, "I'm sorry. You're wrong. What happens in *my* industry is . . ." Instead, just listen. Keep your instant judgments to yourself. Put your thoughts on a new path: "This guy is talking with 'technology language'; let's see if I can find out if his meaning below the words connects with something in the film industry. We're all people doing business. We just juggle different details."

The next element to avoid is defending.

Someone may say, "I see you've made only two films before this. How can I trust that you'll be able to . . ." The reflexive reaction is to defend yourself. At that point, your tone and body tense up. You may even become angry. You must develop a gentle way of deflecting or rerouting that person's comment.

Every semester with my graduate students, I guide them to avoid blocking someone's comment like a karate move. In karate, when one student punches, the other blocks, and both of their arms get bruised. That's force meeting force. That hurts.

A verbal karate block sounds like this:
- "No, that's wrong."
- "That's not true. I am very good at this!"

Instead of using the force–meets–force method of karate, I show my students how to use verbal aikido. Aikido redirects the motion of the attacker rather than opposing it head–on; it is essentially a "flowing out of the way."

The verbal equivalent of an aikido move can sound like this:

- "Sarah, I can hear that you're concerned about _____. And what I can tell you is that my experience in the last years, on eight different movie sets, has been . . . I have seen ____. And I have done_____. And this is how I know, for sure, that I can bring this project in on budget and with good creativity. And let me tell some more about what we're planning here."

Here's something to remember: When a person asks you a question, she is helping you. She is doing you a favor. When you answer her question, you're helping that person decide in your favor. Also, the other investors are thinking, "This presenter is really good at thinking on (his) feet."

Part of preparing a presentation is to prepare your "aikido moves" in advance. The first step in preparing your aikido moves is to identify "The 10 Worst Questions I Do Not Want to Answer." Then write down two answers for each tough question. Then, rehearse your answers. Make sure that your thoughts flow easily when you speak them aloud. You have to be ready for the worst questions.

When it comes to fielding questions from investors, my motto is this: "You can turn a question into a gift, even if it was thrown like a spear."

You do this process when you avoid judging and you avoid defending.

The third element that breaks down listening is the "me, too—one up" trap.

Here's an example. Recently, another instructor at the university where I teach asked me, "How many classes do you teach?"
"Seven," I replied.
"I teach eight!" he said.
"You're tough," I replied.
This instructor's response is an example of "me, too—one up." His tonality and face told me something about his ego. He doesn't

know me; I'm a stranger to him. Yet he needed to be better than me. A better response from him would be: "Seven classes. That can be rough."

Allow the other person to express herself. Avoid the pattern of both commiserating–and–besting the other person. Hear the person out. Be supportive. Show that you're listening and that you're not lost in your own ego.

3. How about sounding flexible?
"Sounding flexible" is the third Power-Three Listening Method. If an investor says something to you, you can respond, "I'll give that a lot of thought." The beauty of this method is that you do *not* need to agree with the investor. You're being flexible by saying that you'll think about the suggestion.

When I sound flexible to my creative team, my team members feel that they can tell me things. That I'm *not* rigid. That I will consider various possibilities, ideas and methods. I'll look at them and sincerely say, "Let me stir that in my soup. Let me ponder that. I'll give that a lot of thought." Perhaps I'll wake up the next morning and call them and say, "I woke up this morning with an idea that goes right along with your suggestion. Thank you. I'm so glad that you brought your idea to my attention."

Your flexibility is part of how team members and investors can trust you. You won't let your own ego get in the way of the best interests of the project. Many investors have been entrepreneurs who have had to often adapt and adjust to things that happen in life. You can start with a business plan, then adapt and adjust and make things turn out even better.

PART 11:
CLEARLY EXPLAIN HOW YOUR FILM CREATES VALUE FOR INVESTORS

Value to each investor is a personal thing. People do not all value the same things. How do you find out what an investor values? You ask good questions. The principle I emphasize is: ***I can't persuade you if I don't know you.***

The point is: I learn about investors by asking good questions.

1. Have you practiced good questions?
Here are examples of good questions:

- "What brings you to consider investing in a film?"
- "So what's most important to you about investing in a film?"
- "What's most important to you about the financials of an offering?"
- "What's most important to you this evening about some of the details I've expressed?"

The form of the question "What's most important to you about . . .?" is truly useful to help you start to understand the values of an investor. When you listen carefully to the investor's answers, you can then tailor your next comments to align with what the investor sees as valuable.

2. Are you repeating a catchphrase?
I was at a particular presentation when a speaker repeated: "Controversy equals money." So the topic of the film was controversial, and it became a firm association in the investors' minds that the film was poised to make them money.

Basically, you want to "say less but say it better." (How about that? Another catchphrase.)

Catchphrases stick in our minds. Many of us remember the phrase "If the glove don't fit, you must acquit" from the O.J. Simpson murder trial of 1995. I saw interviews of several jury members who simply repeated the catchphrase.

Having a catchphrase may be useful in your presentation—something that you repeat three times.

3. Have you repeated the top point three times? (Winston Churchill's "tremendous whack")
Where do you repeat a point? In the introduction of your presentation, the body, and the conclusion.

Winston Churchill said, "If you have an important point to make, don't try to be subtle or clever. Use the pile driver. Hit the point once, then come back and hit it again. Then hit it a third time—a tremendous whack."

I often remind my clients and my graduate students to use "the tremendous whack."

Focus on conveying information in the order that investors want it. You discover the order by asking questions *during* your presentation.

You can begin in this way:

"Thank you so much for being here. It's an honor to present to you today. As I'm beginning here, I was wondering: What's most important to you about a film investment?"

Then you listen and take a few notes. People like it when you take notes because it really means that you're paying attention. You could almost imagine a sign on each person's forehead: "Make me feel important by paying full attention to me."

Incorporate what you learn about your investors' values. For example, you could say, "This film brings to light the ___ topic, which Sarah said is really important to her."

Continue to explain how your film creates value for the investors. By paying attention to your investors, you get to know them; you discover what they value and what they want. And then you show them how your film gives them what they want.

PART 12: HIGHLIGHT UNIQUE, COMPELLING ELEMENTS SO THAT INVESTORS REALLY UNDERSTAND

One of the most powerful things you can do is lead with a story.

1. Can you lead with a story?
When you lead with a story, you're connecting with the person on a primal level of their brain. Researchers often refer to three levels of the human brain:

a) reptile brain (focused on survival)
b) emotional brain (focused on protecting you from loss)
c) neocortex (related to rational thinking)

A story gives an emotional experience, and so it connects with both the reptile and emotional brains.

Experts on persuasion say that a story "gets in under the person's radar." Authors Chris and Dan Heath, in their book, *Made to Stick*, describe a story as "a mental flight simulator." The story gives you an experience. Such an experience can be quite persuasive.

So the idea is to avoid merely presenting facts. Instead, see how you can interweave facts and express them as a story. For example, one could state a fact: "To make the film *Hollywood Shuffle*, writer-director Robert Townsend used credit cards."

Instead, you could tell a story. Something like:

"Writer-director Robert Townsend had two things: skill to make people laugh and a topic that he felt would get African-Americans into the movie theaters. He was so committed to get his film *Hollywood Shuffle* done, he made it by using credit cards. To pay the actors, he used his credit card to fill up the actors' gas tank at the gas station. At this point, he had a third thing: a good story to use in TV interviews to get people to the movie theaters. That's the kind of spirit that runs in our film, *She Knows More*. For publicity, we're not going to talk about credit cards. Instead, we'll talk about . . ."

Tell a story and you have people's attention. A story is one of the compelling elements that I emphasize.

2. Do you ask questions in the beginning? (10 minutes of presentation and 10 minutes of "dialogue")
Earlier, we discussed the value of stories so that you can learn about the investors. I emphasized: "I can't persuade you if I don't know you." Now, I want to emphasize that if you're given only 20 minutes for your presentation, consider "10 minutes of presentation and 10 minutes of 'dialogue'." Avoid presenting/talking at them for all 20 minutes allotted to you.

Simply stated, questions are compelling. They get the investors' attention. Further, the investors' answers are even more compelling. People like to talk and they like to be listened to. Interweave the investors' answers into your presentation. Say something like: "As Janet (an investor) noted, the demographic of 12 to 24 can mean big box office, and..."

Recently, I had a conversation over breakfast with a venture capitalist, and I emphasized the importance of a dialogue with potential investors. He agreed and replied: "Dialogue is scary. People just want to present." I agreed. So you need to prepare yourself. You need to rehearse. You need to think hard about the "10 Questions You Do Not Want to Answer." And you need to come up with at least two answers per tough question.

Here are examples of some tough questions that you might be asked:

- "Isn't investing in film risky?"
- "Isn't it possible that we'll all lose the money and the film won't make a dime of profit?"
- "What if you can't get the film distributed?"
- "What makes you qualified to lead this team? Shouldn't you get an experienced producer to run this project?"

You need to prepare for these and other questions. And to really make your presentation compelling, aim to have a story as part of your answer to any tough question.

PART 13: SECRETS OF CONNECTING TO THE EMOTIONAL BRAIN & WINNING TRUST

We saw in the last section that using stories is a good way to connect with an investor on a primal level—to appeal to that person's reptile brain and emotional brain. Let's explore that topic a bit more and see how we can use this knowledge to improve our pitches.

1. What is the emotional brain programmed for?
Our emotional brain is made up of the amygdala and brain stem. The emotional brain is programmed to avoid loss. A child is born. "There's Mom; I'm hugged and I feel great. Mom just put me down. I feel loss; this is terrible!"

So what do we, as babies, do when we feel loss? We smile; we make noises. We do anything to try to connect so that we don't experience loss.

As adults, we are no different. This reminds me of the old phrase: "If Momma's happy, everybody's happy. If Momma's unhappy, nobody's happy." So people do a lot to keep Momma happy.

They don't want to lose harmony in the family.

We want to connect, we want to be smiled at, and we want someone to listen to us. Most importantly, we want to avoid any sense of loss, which brings me to the next point.

2. Do you clearly show how your offer is strategically designed to avoid loss?
See if you can show that your budget is small enough so that it doesn't take that much to recover the budget plus an additional 20%. Then the investors feel that they will likely *not* lose.

If you are seeking funding from private investors, then you can demonstrate how your project differs from the standard Hollywood–blockbuster pattern. For example, if Hollywood producers make a film for a budget of $100 million and then add another $100 million for prints of the film and advertising, they now have a $200 million investment. To break even, $200 million must be made with domestic and foreign box office proceeds, ancillary markets, and DVD and Blu–ray sales. There is a huge potential for loss here.

Instead, with an independent film, you can show how your budget is designed to avoid loss. You can demonstrate that you have a demographic in which people will come out to see the film. Here's an example: African-American filmmaker Tyler Perry's first feature film, *Diary of a Mad Black Woman*, had a budget of $5.5 million and went on to gross $50.6 million domestically. Subsequent box office history proved that African–American movie theatergoers will go to the movie theater for Perry's comedies. By June 2011, Tyler Perry's films had grossed over $500 million worldwide.

We can look to find the pattern: modest budget plus enthusiastic, reliable, theater–going demographic plus high likelihood of good box office (and later good DVD/Blu-ray sales). Another pattern can be low budget, direct–to–video and direct–to–SyFy Channel films.

PART 14: LEARN WHAT REALLY GETS THE "YES" ANSWER YOU NEED

Years ago, some researchers/authors noted people apparently have input preferences: visual, auditory, and kinesthetic (which I covered earlier in this book). A breakthrough occurred when researchers/authors discovered that decision making actually includes having *three different preferences*: input, processing, and closure. The fastest way I can illustrate this is by talking about how you could sell to me.

In terms of input, I prefer the visual. If you're a salesperson and you call me up and want to have an involved discussion, I'll reply, "Is there a particular webpage? Send me the URL via an email."

When it comes to processing, if you say you'll save me $5,000, I prefer to process it myself with a calculator in my hands. My processing style is kinesthetic (sometimes called "touch").

In the final step of closure, I want to talk with your satisfied clients, so my closure–preferred mode is auditory. I want to talk with people who have known you for years, who are business associates or clients of yours. Ideally, I would like to meet these people face-to-face so that I can watch their expressions.

My profile in summary:

1. Input–visual
2. Processing–kinesthetic
3. Closure–auditory

To really get that "yes" answer from an investor, you need to learn the person's preferred styles of input, processing, and closure.

Do you know how to identify the investor's styles of input, processing, and closure?

This question relates directly to this section's title: "Learn What Really Gets the 'Yes' Answer You Need." Realize that when you align yourself to the *investor's styles of input, processing, and closure,* you put her at ease and inclined to say "yes."

You need to truly listen and observe to pick up clues. For example, if an investor says, "I just got a new BMW." First, congratulate them. Then you can ask, "How did the process go for you? When did you know that this car was the right one for you?"

Possible answers:
- When I sat down and felt the purr of the engine, I knew that this was the car. (kinesthetic)
- When I saw myself at the wheel reflected on the window of the showroom . . . (visual)
- When I heard my business partner say, "Yes, that's the car for you, Joe." (auditory).

PART 15: USE TIME–TESTED SECRETS OF TOP SALESPEOPLE TO HANDLE OBJECTIONS

Over the years, I have trained salespeople, and that resulted in two audio programs: *How Top Salespeople Double Sales in Half the Time and The Best Kept Secrets of Persuasion Masters.* Now, I'll share some of those insights:

1. How do you handle "I'll need to think about it"?
Many investors are likely to say, "I thought it was a good presentation. I'll need to think about it." You can reply, "That's terrific. Thank you. I'm really glad that you'll be thinking about it. Is there anything in particular that you'll be thinking about?" They'll mention one or more details. Then you ask, "Is there anything that I can provide for you that could help you in the process?" You can also ask, "What would you like to know more about?" You avoid letting your thoughts turn negative with something like: "Oh, no. Usual excuse—they're not going to invest."

No! Maybe the person really does need to think about it. Or perhaps they want to talk it over with a trusted advisor or their spouse. You need to be prepared if they say, "I need to talk this over with my CPA (or spouse or lawyer)."

For example, Jake Steinfeld, founder of Body by Jake, went to Aaron Spelling (television mogul) and said, "I would like to invite you to invest in my project." Spelling replied that he needed to talk with his financial advisors. Spelling came back later and said that his advisors had told him that it was not the time to market the project. In his book, Jake Steinfeld left it at that. But now I want to take this a step further. Here's what you do if you need to handle "I need to think about it" or "I need to consult with someone." You can reply with something like: "Sounds good. Oh, do you think that I can have a cup of coffee with you and your CPA?"

Why is this important? No one will be as good a presenter as you are. If you allow the investor to present your story to his advisor, he will not do as well as you can. If the investor presents your offering to his or her spouse, the spouse will likely say, "That doesn't sound so good." Of course, it doesn't...because the investor is not trained to present your offering.

You can present your case with certainty and enthusiasm. Your potential investor can only give a "bad copy." Also, you can answer the advisor's questions in the moment. And let's face it. Things get done when people like each other. You want to meet the advisor face-toface, so that there is the chance that the advisor will like you, too.

2. How do you respond to "Investing in a movie is risky"?
You respond with the truth. You can reply: "Yes. Investing in a movie is risky. And I notice that you're here listening to a number of presentations. So it sounds like you're looking for a project that is worth taking the risk. What makes a film worth it to you? What are you looking for?"

The above sentences are a form of verbal aikido. You are gliding out of the way. You're not trying to do a form of "karate blocking" by saying "No. My film is not risky." Lying like that does not work.

Here's an old phrase that I like to remember: "Can you tell truth to power?" The people with the money have the power. If you pitch effectively, a studio executive or private investors can help change your life. So they have a form of power that you need to respect.

I remember years ago when I had to tell truth to power. I invited a notable person to have an article in one of my books. Later I noticed that out of 300 pages of the book, there was a typo in *his* article. I told him about it. Why? Because I chose to be trustworthy. I said that this mistake happened "on my watch." I resolved that in the next printing the error would be fixed, and it was.

So if you're presenting to investors who are entrepreneurs, they know that mistakes happen. They are impressed by people who take responsibility and express their plan to fix a situation. These responsible people are the ones who can be trusted.

3. Do you have your "evidence" all prepared? (include testimonials, tables, track record, strategic plan)
At one point, when I attended a series of pitches by filmmakers to private investors, I was stunned at how many of them had *neglected* to have testimonials, tables, their track record, and strategic plan all prepared.

You need testimonials. Why? Because hearing other people endorse you and your project heightens your credibility.

If you're using PowerPoint for your presentation, be sure to include videos, too. For example, one presenter had a name actor who had canceled appearing before the investors in person. The presenter said, "He [name actor] wanted to be here, but he's in New York on this new TV series." What was that? Just a bunch of words providing little reassurance to the investors.

Instead, imagine the power if that name actor was featured in a video (even one filmed with a consumer video camera). The name actor could have said, "Hi, I'm [his name]. I'm here on the set of [TV series name]. I so wanted to be there with you today, but the filming schedule is keeping me here in New York. I want you to know that I'm fully committed to this film *Red Engine*, and I have full confidence in Joe Smyth [filmmaker] to make an excellent film. I believe in this movie. And I love this story. When the film's done, I am committed to getting on every possible talk show to promote this film. I'm going to seek out reporters and bloggers. I'm going to promote this film. I invite you to get involved with this film. Thanks for listening."

If I see a video testimonial that reveals an actor's energy, enthusiasm, and confidence in the project and filmmaker, I'm going to feel the truth of the claim that a name actor is on board with the project.

You can convince people with testimonials.

What if you've never made a feature film before? Then have people who know you say things on video like:

- "I know Sarah. She's trustworthy. And she's a great leader. One thing that makes her a great leader is that she works collaboratively and team members tell her what she needs to know so she can make a great decision."

- "I believe this project will be as successful as her short film *Blue Truck* and her other short film *Over the Wall*."

Recently, I consulted with one of my clients on a video that is up on the Internet at various websites. The client had brought a video camera to a major conference during which topline speakers were addressing the crowd. My client knew one of these headliners, who also knew her work. Backstage, she aimed the camera at the name speaker and asked, "Would you say a couple of words about me and about how I help people and that I'm effective doing that." The name speaker said, "Hi, I'm [big name author]. Susan Smith is an excellent speaker. And I believe that Susan can reach your audience and help your people rise to a higher level of performance. So I invite you to call her now and help your team perform at their best."

This endorsement was shot with a little consumer video camera. Amazing! Helpful—and done in two minutes.

PART 16: AVOID THE BIG MISTAKES THAT ARE SURE TO TURN OFF INVESTORS

It's vital that you study and prepare to avoid the big mistakes that can cost you a deal.

1. What bothers investors?
Producers who don't "stay in the game" and carry the risk. If you're the producer, investors expect that you'll carry the risk with them. Their thinking often follows the pattern of "If you don't believe in this project enough to take a risk, then why should I shoulder the risk?" I recall hearing about a top actor who requested a large fee for a film that he wanted to star in. The investors balked at investing in that particular independent feature. Why? They did not want to line the actor's pocket with their money.

The idea is that everyone believes in this express train (the film) and we're all going on it together—and we're all taking the risk.

For example, while making *Titanic,* James Cameron felt slammed by studio executives for going way over budget. In fact, one production associate had hidden a number of receipts in a drawer to the amount of $1 million or more. Cameron said in effect that he believed in the film so much that he was willing to not take a salary. Then, in one meeting, he made it clear that the movie had not gone over budget because they were being careless. Further, he said that he was willing to forego his points of profit participation. He was quite happy that the studio executives did not reduce that statement to writing. He retained his points and made millions from *Titanic*.

See if you can emulate Cameron in a way by saying words to the effect of: "I believe in this movie. I'm not holding back. I'm taking the risk, and you can count on me to give my best and get the best from the cast and crew."

You've got to exude that kind of enthusiasm. That comes from being resolved. On my blog, www.BeHeardandBeTrusted.com, I have written about "I am resolved." That's where the power is. In some military circles, there is a phrase: "Show me your power." When the studio would not pay $5,000 for a breakable window for a moment in *Close Encounters of the Third Kind*, Steven Spielberg paid for it. Investors want to see this level of commitment.

No one demonstrated more power of belief and conviction in filmmaking than Cameron. He even reached into his own pocket to devote his own money to make up the shortfall when the studio refused to pay Kathy Bates her full salary of $500,000 to portray the unsinkable Molly Brown in *Titanic*. Cameron came from the conviction that Kathy was his Molly Brown and that her performance would help make *Titanic* excellent. I agree.

2. Are you coachable?

If you won't listen to their ideas, if you won't write them down for consideration, if you're not coachable, why would investors want to be in a business relationship with you? Potential investors know that arrogant people often lead projects into the ground. Why? People don't like arrogant leaders and they do *not* tell them everything they need to know. Just as bad, arrogant leaders do not learn from other people. The arrogant ones are not coachable. Smart investors will not back people who are not coachable.

3. Do you have a team that fills in your weak areas?
I wrote and published seven books in 2011. How did I do that? With a team. For one book, I had three editors editing different portions of the book simultaneously. I also had a proofreader. Further, I hired a person to typeset the paperback versions of my books.

A powerful phrase that I mention in a number of my books (including *Darkest Secrets of Film Directing*) is: *Know your tendencies and compensate for them*. This means that you, as a great leader, need to know your own tendencies, which include blind spots and weaknesses. A great leader shores up such vulnerable points with team members who are better in those areas. For example, when I do a first edit of a scene, I tend to cut tightly with shots of short duration. So I have other editors take a look. Why? A good film has varying rhythms. Having other people check my work and provide comments is one way that I compensate for my tendencies.

Let your investors know about the notable people on your team. Also, include your circle of advisors.

4. Do you have a script?
There is only one appropriate answer to this question: Yes! Even if you're doing a documentary that will grow and transform throughout post production, you still need to say, "Yes. We have a script." Perhaps the script is only 30 pages, but it does specify locations, topics you will cover and some sample narration. You want to assure the investors that you have a blueprint for what you're doing.

5. Can you avoid "death by PowerPoint"?
You're giving the presentation. PowerPoint is not giving the presentation. PowerPoint is merely a tool. Slides on PowerPoint are merely to back you up. When Steve Jobs was crafting his powerful, persuasive speeches for unveiling new products at

MacWorld, he began with paper and pencil. He did not begin with PowerPoint.

In *Book Four: Improve PowerPoint Presentations*, I'll share eleven techniques to make PowerPoint work for you and support your persuasive presentation.

One of my graduate students prepared a rough draft of his midpoint review speech. This is the crucial speech that helps or hinders him from graduating with a master's degree.

I asked, "How long is your speech?"
"20 minutes," he replied.
"How many slides in PowerPoint are you using?"
"25 slides," he replied.

I pointed out that that was more than one slide per minute, and it appeared that PowerPoint was leading the speech instead of *his* leading the speech. Soon he cut the slides down to 10.

Your audience of investors wants you to convey energy, enthusiasm, and expertise. You need to take center stage. You're the key person that they will trust–or not. When I retitled one of my books as *Be Heard and Be Trusted*, I felt great because that is the heart of my message. You must be heard. Don't try to lean heavily on PowerPoint.

PART 17: CONVERT INVESTORS INTO FANS & SUPPORTERS OF YOU & YOUR FILM

To really gain momentum in a room of investors, you need to go the extra mile. You need to prepare to such a degree that you're going to convert investors into your fans and supporters. Consider the following questions and details:

1. What about you can inspire loyalty?
These details about your virtues and accomplishments can fill various video testimonials.
Here are some sample noteworthy details:

- Sarah is trustworthy.
- Sarah always finishes projects.
- She responds quickly. Of all the people I know, she returns emails and phone calls promptly.
- Sarah tells me the truth, and then together we can fix it.

You need loyalty from your team members and investors. Investors want to know that you're an exceptional leader.

2. Have you noticed that people invest in the person—not just the film?

It's you as a person demonstrating your trustworthiness. Tell stories about how you led a team and accomplished worthy tasks. Share some uplifting comments such as: "That's when Maria, the producer, said, 'I can always count on you, George, to come up with solutions that protect the budget'."

3. What about your film makes it irresistible?(video testimonials, video clips of associated celebrities, teaser trailer, full trailer)
At least do a teaser trailer. Give the investors an *experience* of what is compelling about your film. You're a filmmaker, so show us some film!

The teaser trailer for the film *Trainspotting* included shots that were not in the movie. But the teaser trailer expressed what the movie was about. Laughing, three young guys run down some train tracks. Left behind, their friend (portrayed by a young Ewan McGregor) is tied up on the train track. He says, "Some practical joke, eh? The train will be due any time now... if it's not late, that is." He chuckles. The train's whistle toots in the distance. The guy continues, "Don't smoke—smoking can seriously damage your health. Don't drink and drive. Take plenty of exercise. Don't let drugs screw you up... And don't let your mates tie you to the railway track. Yeah! [Train noise as it's coming closer] Most of all, don't let your mates tie you to the railway track!" He squints his eyes, preparing to get hit by the train.

So what does the viewer get from the video? Young guys doing dopey things. Humor. And there's the reference to "don't let drugs screw you up." The film *Trainspotting* is a 1996 British crime drama that follows a group of heroin addicts in the late 1980s.

The teaser trailer for *The Incredibles* was terrific. I recognized the music, which was from the James Bond film *On Her Majesty's Secret Service* (1969). It's Mr. Incredible, now middle-aged and fat, trying to fasten the belt of his hero suit. His wife calls out, "Honey, come to dinner." And he replies, "I can't come to dinner . . . maybe a salad and some rice cakes." This scene from the trailer was *not* in the movie, but it gave investors a good idea of what to expect in the full version of the film.

So use a teaser trailer perhaps by filming one short sequence.

If you have a guest star, you can have a video in which he says, "Hi, I'm [celebrity name], and I'm looking forward to being in this movie because I really believe in this [topic]. So thank you for investing in this film."

Show storyboards and produce an animatic (storyboards strung together as a sequence with minimal animation).

George Lucas got a big "yes" from 20th Century Fox studio executive Alan Ladd, Jr. by showing paintings that depicted scenes of *Star Wars* (*Episode IV: A New Hope*—the first film produced). Now, over 34 years later, I still recall one painting in particular of Darth Vader in a swordfight (with lightsabers). That image captured the magic and wonder of the *Star Wars* film project.

Show as much as you can. Another way to demonstrate your marketing savvy is to talk about how you'll have two versions of the DVDs/Blu–rays: a standard version and an "unrated" version of the film. Make mockups of the DVD and Blu–ray packaging. If your budget is low and you can't afford a professional graphic artist, you can provide a modest fee to a college student. You could even hold a contest and pay the winner a fee to complete the project.

This reminds me of one of the most powerful presentations that I have ever heard. Years ago, a guy with an idea waited outside when a line of others presented to a group of venture capitalists. He noticed that the others all had well–prepared slide presentations. But he was not prepared. When he got into the room, he pulled a little book from his briefcase. He tossed the book onto the table and said, "My device will be this small." One investor picked up the book and said, "You can't make a computer this small." (Keep in mind this was many years ago, before iPads and smart phones.) Another investor grabbed the book and said,

"No, Glenn, he could do it by using . . ." Another investor said, "I know a company that has a processor that could be placed in there."

The investors basically convinced themselves, and the guy walked out of the room with pledges of $3 million to pursue his project. He got the investors involved. He showed them something. He gave them something that they could touch and that they could look at. That's one reason for making mockups of the DVD and Blu–ray packaging.

The above is the process of making your film irresistible.

PART 18: PREPARE AN EFFECTIVE POST–PITCH FOLLOW-UP STRATEGY

Your relationship with the investors only begins at the presentation. Often, you must follow–up to finally get signatures and checks.

1. Do you have an "Up–the–Steps" plan? (In other words, do you have a plan to guide the investor to 'yes'?)
You must figure out the steps that the investors need to ascend until they finally give you a check. First, filmmakers often create a private placement memorandum (PPM) of a limited partnership. A PPM is used to:

a) present the positive aspects of the film project.
b) present all potential risks to the investor.
c) protect the filmmaker in case the project fails in some way.
d) comply with all national and state regulations for such an offering.

So Step One is that the investor accepts the PPM and agrees to look at it. By the way, depending on what your offering is, you can only give out a certain number of copies of the PPM to "sophisticated investors." You'll need to check with your attorney about many related details. Some definitions of "sophisticated investors" hold that a sophisticated investor has either a net worth of $2.5 million or has earned more than $250,000 in the past two years. Again, check with your attorney.

Just because you give someone the PPM does not mean that he's going to read the whole thing because he's probably busy doing his own business. So you need to guide him to read it and to give you a follow–up appointment with him. You also need to think about what additional information you can give him. If you have a big name actor involved, perhaps you can send the potential investor a follow–up video clip of the actor addressing him and encouraging him to finish looking over the paperwork.

If someone is going to buy 10 units ($5,000 each), you may want to have the name actor give a phone call to the potential investor.

What are your personal steps so that you guide the investor to sign the check? Write them down. Make your own Up–the–Steps Plan.

Here's a side note: Avoid handing someone an agreement and saying, "Will you sign this?" Instead, say, "Would you okay this?" That wording is more comfortable to the person. People tend to have some subconscious fears about "signing their life away."

Special Note: You must "ask for the order."

This means you must literally ask the person to invest. You can say something like: "So are you ready to invest now? Would you like to do the paperwork?"

Other ways to invite the person to sign include:
- "How about we go forward with this?"
- "So you're ready to do this right now?"

You need to ask again and again (in different ways). According to research, it takes five impressions before a person buys something. I realize that this may feel uncomfortable. Recently, I was having coffee with a person, and I had to push myself to say, "So you mentioned yesterday that you wanted to buy [quantity] of books. I have them in my car. So we're ready to make this happen."

2. What Contact Management Software do you use?
With every conversation with an investor, you'd do better to log the details. Where? In your contact management program. You need to know where the person is in your Up-the-Steps Plan. You need to know what promises you have made. Did you promise to send him an article about films that do similar business to your proposed film? You want your calendar system to send you alerts of your next move. For example, I use Google Calendar, and I have it send me an email reminder to do certain vital activities. You may want to have a mobile device like an iPhone or a BlackBerry so that you can have a phone conversation and then immediately send a follow–up email with an attached document.

Keep all the potential investors in the loop. You can send out updates. What I've noticed with my own projects is that they become like express trains. They gain momentum, and then people say, "It's already going. I'll get on board."

For updates, you can provide a website and brief email updates. Use video because, according to research, people often prefer to see a video rather than to read something. The idea is for potential investors to feel that the project is an express train and there's nothing that will derail it. They'll feel safe. You need to demonstrate confidence so that potential investors can think: "I can participate or not. This project is going to go on without me."

You want an air of inevitability to grace your project. It will get done with quality in a reasonable time. There's no doubt about it. We have a strong leader with vision and good business relationships, so the film will be completed on a level of excellence.

3. What is your fail–proof system to overcome procrastination?
If you want something to get done, you need to measure it. For

example, as of the moment I typed the previous sentence, I had 16,059 words of this book completed. I measure my daily writing progress. If you set the goal of contacting 20 potential investors in the month of May, then you need a system to get the next step done *no matter what*. Set up what I call *Effort–Goals* like:

- I will set up 8 meetings–in–person per week
- I will send out 12 emails per week

Procrastination can arise with these three situations:
a) You do not know what to do next.
b) You do not know how to do something.
c) You feel that in some way the task is "going to hurt" or at least feel uncomfortable.

In my book, *Nothing Can Stop You This Year, 2nd Edition*, I cover a whole system called the G.O.–N.O.W. system to overcome procrastination. Here are a couple of the details:

1. Keep score and achieve more
To make sure you keep moving forward, you need to keep score. Find someone who cares about you and the project, and tell them, "I made 10 phone calls today, and my target is to make 12 calls tomorrow." Then add, "On Friday, my target is to send email messages to 7 potential investors."

2. Get the pain out
What's the first thing that gets us to procrastinate? The anticipation of pain. So make strategic moves. Find a way to get the pain out. For example, one of my clients, Trudy, had a friend hold her hand when she made her first "cold calls" toward getting funding for her film. She needed support, and she took action to get that support. She took the potential pain out of making those cold calls.

3. Nurture rewards
You can't wait for someone else or the world to reward you. You need to take charge of rewarding yourself. In some ways, your "inner child" is the source of your energy. So if you set up a

reward, it's almost like your inner child gets on board and says, "Sure. Here's the energy. I'm looking forward to that new DVD." I call this process "giving yourself 'Self–Rewards'."

Summary of Book Two:

1. You need to take care of golden time (the time before you actually make the presentation). You need to connect with the investors before you formally present.

2. Make that connection. If someone offers you coffee, say yes. And just sip the coffee if you're not into coffee. Talk with the person near the coffeemaker (if that's the situation). Talk with people. Listen to them. Make the connection.

3. When you're making a presentation, make it a "dialogue." Face the person who asks you a question. Remember my phrase: "Heart faces heart." Lean forward slightly, and your body will help you listen better.

4. Focus on this idea: *I can't persuade you if I don't know you.* You need to ask gentle questions even during your presentation. Have a dialogue with the potential investors. Make it a person-to-person connection.

5. People don't invest just in projects; they invest in the person. For example, Ross Perot invested in Steve Jobs, along with Jobs' company NeXT.

Now, we'll move onto *Book Three: Use the P.I.T.C.H. Process.*

BOOK 3

In some ways, this section will summarize material in other parts of this book. Each semester I guide college students and graduate students in what I call the P.I.T.C.H. process:

P – prepare your questions for them
I – intrigue with "how you came up with the idea"
T – target where they live
C – cut the presentation down and invite questions
H – help the person "into the room"

USE THE P.I.T.C.H PROCESS

1. Prepare your questions for them
Many people think that a pitch is all about what one says. In many cases, the most effective pitch is a dialogue. Before you start your presentation, you may have the opportunity to engage a potential investor in small talk. Small talk often involves asking questions. Situations vary. It depends on who you are pitching to.

To a Studio Executive:

Pitch–maker: So how's today going for you?
Studio Executive: Intense. One of our stars just had a meltdown. So what do you got for me?
(Pitch–maker makes the pitch.)
Studio Executive: Sounds like that would work, but we already have four action movies going. What else have you got?
Pitch–maker: Is there a genre that's a hole in your schedule? Something you're looking for?

To a Private Investor:

Pitch–maker: So how do you come to this meeting? Are you looking for something in particular for an investment in a film?

To a Name Actor:

Name actor: So do you have any actors attached already?
Pitch–maker: [Actor's name] is on board. I'm wondering. Is there a kind of role that you've been itching to do?

Who controls a conversation? The person asking the questions. Make sure that you prepare and rehearse questions that guide the person to say, "Yes."

2. Intrigue with "how you came up with the idea"
It truly helps to tell the person how you came up with the idea first. Why? Because often you run into times when the person does *not* give you her full attention at the beginning of the interaction. Similarly, various screenplay consultants suggest that you do *not* mention the name of the film first. Instead, get the person's attention by saying something like: "First, let me share how I came up with this idea. I was standing at a curb when I started to take a step into the street. Suddenly, I got this feeling to pull back. Good thing—a car ran a red light. As I caught my breath, sure I'd just missed getting killed, I had the idea: What if a guy had the ability to . . ."

At this point, you have the person's attention, and you can talk about the actual story of your film.

3. Target where they live
People say a lot of things. So how do you know what their real values are? Look at their behaviors. An old phrase is: "It's not what you say; it's what you do." When I say "target *where they live*," I mean find out what is most important to them.

Before you meet with a studio executive, see if you can do some "detective work" and find out what types of films the executive has been involved with. At least look the person up on imdb.com and do a Google search. During your Internet searching, see if you can find out if the person is involved in any charity work. Sometimes, people volunteer because they have a real connection to a topic or issue. See if you can find any interviews (video–recorded or written on some website) which may give you clues as to whether a studio executive has deep convictions about her charity work. If your film relates to something the person is interested in, you may have a leg up.

4. Cut the presentation down and invite questions

A number of venues exist in which a filmmaker can address a group of private investors. Often, the investors view five to seven pitches in a row. If you are allotted only twenty minutes, consider presenting for ten minutes and having a discussion (taking questions) for ten minutes. Without hearing the potential investors' questions, you will not know what is important to them. Further, if you know what they value, you can tailor the rest of your presentation around their values. You could say, "Sarah mentioned that she wanted to invest in films that inspire young people, and our film *She Knows More* is just such a film. For example, the story focuses on . . ."

5. Help the person "into the room"

Author and screenplay consultant Michael Hauge advises, "Don't lead with your title." Why not? Because the person is likely "not in the room yet." That means, the person is still thinking about whatever happened just before you sat down in his office (a phone call, an argument, who knows?).

So your first job is to help the person "get into the room"—that is, to pay attention to you and your project. One way, as mentioned above, is to talk about how you came up with the idea.

Since we began with Hauge's admonishment to not lead with your title, let's continue with further mistakes that Hauge advises you to avoid:

1. Don't lead with a question.
2. Don't lead with a logline.
3. Don't name all your characters.
4. Don't use jargon.
5. Don't give away the ending.
6. Don't hype your story.

7. Don't try to tell your entire story.

Now, I'll share my thoughts on Hauge's suggestions:

1. Don't lead with a question
There's controversy on this one. As a public speaker, I ask questions often during my presentations. Why? It engages the listener. (I'm sure you also noticed that I just asked a question.) However, Hauge does have a point. If you ask something like: "Do you ever wonder what happened to your high school prom date?" That question is too compelling as Hauge points out. The listener will disappear into positive or negative memories.

What to do? Be strategic about the question. Ask a question that may spark some interest, but avoid questions that derail your pitch. Or skip the question routine completely, and just flow into something like: "Let me start with how I came up with this idea . . ."

2. Don't lead with a logline
A logline is like shorthand for what a film is about. The problem is that it is so short and curt that it can leave out the "flavor" of your unique story. A logline sounds like: "A New York City cop travels to Los Angeles to reconcile with his wife but learns she's been taken hostage by terrorists in a skyscraper—and he struggles alone to save her. It's called *Die Hard*." (as said by WME Story Editor Christopher Lockhart)

Hauge's longtime friend and associate Devora Cutler–Rubenstein invites writers to *end* their pitch with the logline. Great idea! You give the flavor of the story first, and then you summarize the story with the industry's standard tool: the logline. This reveals that you're a savvy member of the industry—or at least, you've done your homework.

3. Don't name all your characters

Imagine hearing a pitch like:

So this is a story about Sam who's a high school teacher who helps Aaron win the heart of sassy Brenda before her brother George takes on the . . .

At any point, the studio executive will be saying: "What? Who? Who's the hero of this story?"

If you feel it will help create appropriate feelings in the listener, name just the hero.

4. Don't use jargon

Every author of a book on screenwriting uses different jargon. If you talk about plot points, rising action, the "save the cat" scene, the "pet–the–dog" scene, the "returns with the elixir" moment, then you are getting away from your story. Just tell your story with enthusiasm and precision.

5. Don't give away the ending

Why not? You want the studio executive to be in suspense so that she'll read your screenplay! Or at least give it to her reader to read the screenplay. Just telling someone the ending may get the response of "Yeah, I thought so. That's how these types of movies end." Or maybe "That's lame. The audience will hate that."

There is an exception here. If the studio executive asks you for the ending, just tell her. Don't play games. At least she's interested enough to ask.

6. Don't hype your story

Good point! If you say something like: "This is the best premise for an action film since *Die Hard,*" the studio executive is primed to resist. She'll probably think something like: "Yeah? I'll be the judge of that!" Just tell your story and get the person to experience it. Immediately comparing your story to something that has already been produced only creates "noise" that may obscure your idea.

Now, some studio executives do insist on reducing everything to "It's *Alien* meets *Annie Hall,* on a *Midnight Express* to Funky

Town." If the studio executive does that, listen. Then add something like: "And the twist is . . . And this would likely appeal to audiences that liked . . ."

7. Don't try to tell your entire story

Studio executives (and just about everyone nowadays) have short attention spans. You have about one to two minutes to deliver the best of your pitch. So avoid trying to tell the whole story. Come on! Your script is 90 pages to 110 pages. At one page a minute, it would take way too long to tell the whole story. Just tell the most compelling parts of your story.

To give yourself an extra edge, consider memorizing the elements of the P.I.T.C.H. process. You can even test yourself on the morning before giving a pitch. Take out a sheet of paper and write P.I.T.C.H. Then write down what each letter stands for. Finally, write down your film's particular elements that fit in the P.I.T.C.H. categories. Good! You'll be more prepared than many other people pitching their projects.

BOOK 4

One phrase I've heard is: "Avoid death by PowerPoint." This means that many people have given terribly boring PowerPoint demonstrations which feel to the audience like a slow death. I've survived a couple of them myself.

Realize that you are not required to use PowerPoint. In fact, some top pitch-makers use printed boards resting on stands because the images will not disappear from a screen like a PowerPoint slide. If you decide to use PowerPoint, the following material will help you. you keep your audience's attention. Some of the material below was inspired by the work of author Jeffrey Gitomer and by my own experiences.

P – point size of 44
O – one point per slide
W – white background
E – energize with a video (testimonial)
R – refrain from using "movement"
P – power up words with a red color and/or a larger font size
O – one laugh per 5 slides
I – inquire (ask a question)
N – no silly clipart (instead use a photo)
T – tell a story with the slides

IMPROVE POWERPOINT PRESENTATIONS

1. Point size of 44
First, you do not have to use the font point size of 44 every time. The idea here is to use a large font. Jeffrey Gitomer likes to use the font style of *Impact*. Others do not. When you use a large font size, though, you'll likely keep the material on your slide to one sentence. That's a good idea. Which leads us to the next method . . .

2. One point per slide
Stating one idea or point per slide is clear and concise. Remember, the PowerPoint slide is used to *back up* what you're saying, not overtake it. You and your message are center stage. Some people destroy their presentation by listing five points before they get to them. Then the audience is ahead, and they're bored. Instead, plan on one point per slide.

3. White background
We've been conditioned to read black printing on white paper. There is a comfort in this. So when you place your text on a white background, you're tuning into this comfort. Contracts also have black printing on a white background, so the impression is "This is important." Plus, some people have vision issues, and black–on–white provides the greatest amount of contrast with the least amount of distraction.

4. Energize with a video (testimonial)
I mentioned the value of using a video testimonial in a number of places in this book. Using a video testimonial gives the investor the experience of "seeing is believing." If you, the presenter, say that a name actor is attached to your project, it is just words. But if the investor sees, via video, the name actor express his commitment to the project, you establish true credibility.

5. Refrain from using "movement"
The worst PowerPoint presentation I have ever seen (so far) included text zooming across the screen with the roar of a race car. After two times, I looked at the faces in the audience, and it was apparent that many of us were dreading more movement and repetitive sounds. Instead, have text just "pop up" on the screen. Don't waste the audience's time waiting for something to move or slowly fade in. We're used to fast cuts in current movies.

6. Power up words with a red color and/or a larger font size
When you want someone to see a word stand out from other words, you can use the color red. Also, you could decide to make the word larger. When would this be useful? Imagine the sentence "Here are benefits for you, the investor." You could decide to emphasize the word "benefits" or "you." Your choice. Using a color change or an increase in font size is a way to simulate how a person emphasizes a word in conversation.

7. One laugh per 5 slides
Jeffrey Gitomer suggests having a funny image after five slides. You need to be careful here. No bit of humor works for everyone in the room. Also, it hurts you if the humorous image is off topic. It pulls the investor's attention away from your important points. And yet, I remember this quote:

Among those whom I like or admire, I can find no common denominator, but among those whom I love, I can: All of them make me laugh.—W.H. Auden

So if you have some skills related to humor, they can give you an edge.

8. Inquire (ask a question)
Questions are better than just bullet points with statements. Let's say you have a slide that reads: "Women live longer than men." The brain immediately takes on that statement. *Does that make sense? Do I believe that?*

Instead, use a question like: "Why do women live longer than men?" Now, you have engaged a different part of the brain. In fact, your audience will now be helping you to find answers that support the question. So if possible, consider making some questions from your one point slides.

9. No silly clipart (instead use a photo)
David Ogilvy, considered the father of modern advertising and founder of the company that later became Ogilvy & Mather, preferred photos over illustrations. In fact, decades later, I still remember the cover of his acclaimed book *Confessions of an Advertising Man*. The cover had a *photo* of a book with the title *Confessions of an Advertising Man.*

So drop silly clipart. Everyone has seen clipart, and they're tired of the images. Many people look with disdain at such clipart images.

10. Tell a story with the slides
Every great presentation uses storytelling. How do you tell a story with slides?
Imagine that you use slides like this:

Slide 1: What do you want in a film investment opportunity?

Slide 2: How is *Red Engine* a good film investment?

Slide 3: How will you get a number of benefits from your investment in *Red Engine*?

The above slides would support the story that investors would be smart to invest in the film *Red Engine.*

Bonus Tip: Add a logo to the lower corner.

Having a logo for your company gives the feeling of a stable organization behind the film investment offering. Now, you can give a subtle message to the potential investor's subconscious mind. Every slide can show your company logo in the bottom left corner. The logo will not be obtrusive, but it will be ever–present. Certainly, make sure that your logo is of high quality.

BOOK 5

Each semester I guide college students and graduate students in what I call the Q.U.I.C.K. process for answering tough questions in a "questions and answers" session:

Q – qualify and "do not accept the premise"
U – understand the *3 Steps*: Catch the question, Answer the question, Shine light on the diamond
I – include *your* question
C – control the session with "And then I will summarize."
K – keep to the truth when you don't know the answer

HOW TO ANSWER TOUGH QUESTIONS

1. Qualify and "do not accept the premise"

One definition of *qualify* is "to pronounce fit or able" or "to label something unfit." When you qualify a question, you make a decision whether that question will help you or not. Imagine this question:

"How do you have the gall to ask us to invest in this film when your last film did not earn a dime?"

That question sounds harsh. Do *not* accept the premise that it takes gall to present a new film investment offering.

The solution is to provide an answer that gets at the investor's concern and still avoids hurting yourself. Here's a possible answer:

"George, I can see that you're concerned about this. And what I can say is that in the three years since that project, I have been vice president at XY Company. During that time, I have been doing _______ and I have learned _________."

We live in a world of sound bites and cameras in people's phones. You do *not* want to hurt yourself by agreeing to some detrimental statement. Avoid saying anything like: "I hear you, George. Yes, I failed with that last film . . ."

For one thing, it may *not* be true. For example, *The Princess Bride* is a quality film that did little business at the box office. However, it became a hit on VHS tape, then on DVD, and recently on Blu-ray as parents introduce the film to their children. So if director Rob Reiner had said, "I failed with *The Princess Bride*," that would have proved untrue. Sometimes, a film is a quality effort, but there may be various factors that make the marketplace not ready for it.

So carefully answer a tough question. See if you can get at the underlying concern that the investor may hold.

2. Understand the *3 Steps*: Catch the question, Answer the question, Shine light on the diamond

Here are the 3 Steps of Answering a Tough Question:

1. Catch the Question
2. Answer the Question
3. Shine Light on the Diamond

Now, I will guide you through the process:

1. Catch the Question
Each semester, I tell my graduate students: "You can turn a question into a gift even if it was thrown like a spear."

Then I show them a pillow and say, "Imagine that this small pillow is made of Kevlar (bullet-proof material). Next, imagine that this pen is a spear. See how the pillow can catch the pen. And the pen does not get through to hurt me. I've just demonstrated the process of 'Catch the Question.'"

To "catch the question," you can use replies like:
- That's a good question. I'm glad you brought that up.
- George, I can see that's important to you.
- I haven't looked at it quite that way before. I'll need to pause for a moment because I want my answer to be valuable to you.

The point is that you demonstrate that you're not ruffled by the question. You show your confidence and capability.

2. Answer the Question

The next step is to answer the question. If we flip through cable TV channels, we see people skip answering questions every day. They just jump to the "talking points" (the things *they* want to talk about). They use clumsy transitions like: "Bob, that's not the real question. The real point is: Now is not the time for finger pointing." These people who are avoiding questions are *not* fooling a significant number of viewers. And they're *not* convincing many people either.

Instead, you need to answer the question. How? Let's go back to an example I shared earlier in this book:

Tough Question: "How do you have the gall to ask us to invest in this film when your last film did not earn a dime?"

The answer: "George, I can see that you're concerned about this. And what I can say is that in the three years since that project, I have been vice president at XY Company. During that time, I have been doing _______ and I have learned _________. I now know about a segment of the marketplace that would love a film like *She Knows More*."

3. Shine Light on the Diamond

The final step is to "shine light on the diamond," which means that you *talk about what you want to emphasize*. The metaphor is that you have something valuable to offer ("the diamond") and with a flashlight you bring it to the investors' attention.

As I mentioned earlier, some clumsy speakers avoid answering the investors' questions. It's only after you've caught the question and answered the question that you've "earned the right" to express what you want to emphasize. Let's face it. Investors hate it when the speaker is "slippery." Instead, demonstrate that you're trustworthy. Answer questions—and then speak on your "talking points."

3. Include *your* question
As mentioned previously, it's important to make your pitch into a dialogue. For example, if you ask, "Are there any questions so far?" and no one responds, here's something you can do. You can say, "I have a question for you. 'What's most important to you about a film investment?'" As I have said a number of times in this book: *I can't persuade you if I don't know you*. So preparing your questions ahead of time helps you learn about the potential investors. You are seeking their "hot button"—what really moves their feelings so that they want to invest in your film. Once you know someone's hot button, you can go back to it during your presentation. For example, Alison Bechdel wrote a comic that included what has become known as the Bechdel Test.

The Bechdel Test (about a film's content):
1. There are two female characters
2. Who talk to each other
3. About something other than a man.

If one of your potential investors is a woman who mentions the Bechdel Test and your film features fully developed women characters, then you can mention how your film is one of the few films that actually passes the Bechdel Test. You could even ask the question, "Sarah, did you notice how my film *She Knows More* passes the Bechdel Test?"

4. Control the session with "And then I will summarize"
Avoid ending your presentation simply with a question and answer session. Why? Because you lose momentum and power. When I gave presentations at six annual National Association of Broadcasters Conferences in Las Vegas, I noticed how many other presenters' speeches ended with a question and answer session that puttered to a lame stop. The speaker would say plaintively, "Does anyone else have a question? Well . . . uh . . . I guess that's it. Uh . . . thanks."

Here is the powerful way to control a question and answer session.

Speaker: "In a moment, I can take a few questions and then I will summarize. Who has the first question? . . . [after a few questions] Who has the last question? . . . . And now I will summarize."

Then, the speaker makes a big, positive impact by reminding the audience of the most important benefits and excellent features she mentioned during the earlier portion of her pitch. She ends with power.

5. Keep to the truth when you don't know the answer

People are sharp, and they often pick up subtle clues when someone is lying. So save yourself from disaster. Do not make up answers when you don't know the details.

I'll give you two scenarios.

Scenario 1: A screenwriter pitches to a studio executive

Joe completes his pitch, and then the studio executive asks, "What's the budget for this?"

Joe responds, "I could make a wild guess. But I'm really a storyteller. I'm sure you and a line producer could come up with a great budget."

Scenario 2: A film producer pitches to a potential investor

The investor asks, "Do you really think that the marketplace will make *She Knows More* a hit movie?"

The producer, Stephanie, responds, "We've designed this film to have lots of laughs and some thrilling moments to get the audience to gasp. Our director has a good track record of making films that appeal to the 12 to 24–year–old segment of the market. I can't be sure that the marketplace will do what we hope. But our team has certainly done our homework."

The point is that studio executives and potential investors are sharp people. They can see through lies. In fact, get caught in a lie, and you burn a bridge.

If an investor asks a question and you can later look it up, it's an opportunity for you to follow up with them.

Imagine being forthright and saying, "Mira, that's a good point. I don't have that statistic at the moment. But I'll look that up and send you a follow–up email within 24 hours."

Just make sure that you don't trip over yourself trying to please people. Be straight forward and strong. Tell the truth.

BONUS SECTION

In this bonus section, we have the opportunity to explore an overview of further material that I've written to empower people who want to make big dreams come true.

We will cover these topics/questions:

1. How do you seize attention in a conversation?
2. How do you improve your confidence?
3. How do you handle fear?
4. How do you keep going despite disappointment and frustration?
5. How can you make sure to have enough personal energy to excel?
6. How can you overcome procrastination and make significant progress?
7. What is the essence of enhancing business and personal relationships?

1. HOW DO YOU SEIZE ATTENTION IN A CONVERSATION?

First, I coach my clients and graduate students to ask an easy question so the other person will talk about themselves. They'll enjoy expressing themselves and being heard by you. My phrase is: When you're listening, you're winning.

When it's time for you to express something about yourself, use the power of story.

Pull with a Story

"Tell me a story!" Millions of children throughout the world say this every day. A story gives us an experience. The story reaches us on our subconscious and emotional levels. The story goes around people's natural resistance.

We have been conditioned to respond favorably to stories. With a dash of suspense, tension, and release, your story can influence your listener.

If you can dream it, you can do it. —Walt Disney

It all comes down to the story you tell yourself. —Tom Marcoux

Facts go in our brains. Stories go in our hearts.—Sandra Bloch

A good story …
1. Begins with a grabber
2. Has suspense
3. Has vivid details
4. Includes word pictures
5. Ends with "What I learned was … "
6. Has a call to action

A *word picture* creates an image. To a friend who likes puppies, I said, "When I'm waiting for you, I feel like a puppy on a raft in the middle of the Atlantic Ocean, never knowing whether a rescue ship is going to appear." My comment touched her heart.

A story with a goal gives us the chance to earn the ending. We go through the trials and suffering along with the main character.

Character cannot be developed in ease and quiet.
Only through experience of trial and suffering
can the soul be strengthened, vision cleared,
ambition inspired, and success achieved.—Helen Keller

We want to earn the happy ending. We want to see how the hero with good intentions struggles and then earns the positive outcome.

A story helps you make your point powerfully. The following anecdote is one of the signature stories I tell my audiences.

> "We need to be careful about the stories we tell ourselves–and the stories we tell others. At one point, my wife and I went on the Disney Cruise. We went to refresh ourselves, and I also went on the cruise to find more stories. "I need a story," I felt. "I need an adventure."
>
> When I was younger, I did stunts. I'd hang on the hood of a

a speeding truck, a cherry-red classic Chevy truck going 60 miles an hour. Not any more! So now I need an adventure.

Let's go on a cruise and go snorkeling for the first time! It looked good on paper. So I go snorkeling with my sweetheart. It's the Bahamas, and it's 83 degrees at eight o'clock in the morning. It's hot, so she tells me that the water will be warm. But the water is relatively cold. And I discover what happens in cold water. First thing I learn: What is worse than a cramp in your right leg?

"A cramp in both legs," says an audience member.

Yes! You're right here with me. A cramp in both legs. So now I have terrible, horrible pain that I cannot solve with a "to–do" list or a "guilt" list. I cannot solve this by doing it harder—"Let's move the legs harder!"

It looks like a mile back to the beach. I've got to let go. I've got to relax. I've got legs that don't work, and they hurt like fire. So I start to use my arms. Thank goodness for Red Cross swimming lessons! I do the sidestroke. And my sweetheart–yes, she's better at snorkeling her first time than I am. (Women in the audience laugh.) She's towing me a little bit, too. That's comforting.

"Eventually, we get back to the ship and our cabin. And I discover the second thing that happens in cold water: things shrink! (Audience chuckles.) My hand has shrunk. My wedding–ring finger has shrunk. (Audible gasps.)

My wedding ring is now lost in hundreds of yards of water and sand. My wedding band is gone! And I'm thinking, All right, I teach this stuff. Mental discipline. My ring has gone back to the universe. Someone will find it who needs it more than I. (Audience laughs.)

I have had this ring for seven years. It has served me well. It is time for a change. I will flow. I teach about Taoism in my Comparative Religion class. I will flow. Be like water! The ring is in the water. It is in the sand; it is not on my hand. I discovered: All men make mistakes; married men just find out about it sooner. (Audience laughs).

My wife tells me, "You do not go into water with jewelry on!" I am not into jewelry–and now jewelry is not on me!

So I call up the ship's Guest Services and say, "My wedding ring is somewhere in hundreds of yards of sand and water." The person says that I can come by and fill out the form. There's always a form. There's a form for losing your wedding ring.

The next day, I go to the Guest Services desk. I'm thinking, "It's okay. It's all right. I've had it for seven years (whimper of sadness)." So I talk with a new person at the Guest Services desk. "I'm here to fill out the form. I lost my wedding ring."

"Where did you lose it?" he asks me.

"I was on the island tram. And I was at the snorkeling lagoon …"

"Is this your ring?" (Audience gasps.)

And here is the ring. (I hold up my hand with the wedding ring.)

To me, it is a miracle. And it reminds me of what
Albert Einstein said:
"There are two ways to live: you can live as if nothing is a miracle; you can live as if everything is a miracle."

We have a choice. And so, what are the stories you are telling yourself? What are the stories you tell others?

Are you telling yourself stories so that you can have a year where *nothing can stop you this year*?*"

You can see how this snorkeling-adventure story illustrates my point about the stories we tell ourselves and others. Be careful about the stories you tell yourself and the stories you tell others.

NOTE: * This is an excerpt from my speech related to my book *Nothing Can Stop You This Year*!

Tell Good Stories–Miraculous Stories

I often tell audiences, "Just about everyone in this room has a good story about something that went well–a lucky break, a miracle, even like when you're thinking about someone and the person calls you on the phone." Then I invite the audience to place their hands over their hearts and feel their hearts beating. Finally, the audience joins me in saying the four powerful words Dr. Martin Luther King, Jr., shared with us all: "I have a dream."

Remember to pull the listener in with a good story.

Principle:
Use a story to eliminate resistance.

Power Question:
What stories can seize the attention of your listener?

(The above is an excerpt from my book, *Be Heard and Be Trusted)*

2. HOW DO YOU IMPROVE YOUR CONFIDENCE?

"I won't try that until I feel comfortable about it," and other versions of this statement pop up in our daily lives.

Another limiting statement is "That won't work for me; I don't feel confident about doing that."

When these kinds of statements run a person's life, he or she may be paralyzed into a dis–empowering life. A life of routine. Perhaps, with fewer lows, but unfortunately with the absence of true joy and exhilaration. But this is *not* for you.

I've studied and trained in methods to improve confidence. Why? Since I was a nine–year–old, I've wanted big, positive things. And I discovered that I'd have to do extraordinary things to make my dreams come true. I'm not talking from theory. This is real world experience here!

I've learned that two elements arise related to confidence:
a) experiencing "true confidence" that inspires valuable action
b) feeling confident.

Related to experiencing true confidence, you need to shift from "I need to feel comfortable" to "I only need to feel capable enough."

trait: they did NOT wait to feel comfortable before taking action.

In my book *10 Seconds to Wealth: Master the Moment Using Your Divine Gifts*, I revealed the W.A.K.E. process of true confidence. I'll provide a brief summary and a few significant details to begin this discussion.

Want it from Your True Self

To feel confident, you need energy. But if your goal is not your own, then you may find that you just don't feel like making the effort. Your True Self is the source of real personal energy. Your True Self is that part of you that is naturally brilliant and courageous. Many authors and spiritual teachers suggest that your True Self is connected to Higher Power or the goodness of the universe. How exciting and empowering! I've experienced that in my own life. I wanted so much to make films that I stepped away from feeling shy to push myself out in front of people to lead them in making my films. I remember my high school days leading 17 of my fellow students in a fight scene while I made a film called *True Hero*. Some of the kids were bigger than me, and others had greater standing at the school, but my desire to create a film filled me with energy and courage.

Now I ask you: What do you want? What is something from deep in your heart? To experience true confidence, one born of strong personal energy, you need to start with a desire that is stronger than fear.

Courage is not the absence of fear, but rather the judgment that something else is more important than fear.—Ambrose Redmoon

Your desire from your True Self is more important than fear.

Adapt

If you know that you can roll with whatever comes along, that's a great source of confidence and emotional strength. To be reading these words, you have likely adapted to plenty of things so far in life. Now, take those experiences and fortify your feelings of being capable.

In interviewing successful people, I've seen a big difference. Many of them keep their accomplishments (especially those that involved adapting) front and center in their mind. They remind themselves that they are capable and have the capacity to adapt to whatever new things arise.

Keep on Learning

No matter what we know or have experienced, a new situation brings new opportunities and new problems. We can use this principle: When you're learning, you're winning. In over twenty years of doing projects (feature films, songs, feature film music soundtracks, audio programs, and books), I have learned with each project. Sometimes when I look back, I wish I had known more while doing a particular project. But then I remember: *We learn by doing.* If you're okay with learning and training before you begin a new project, and you're prepared to learn while you're doing the project, you will have a foundation of solid confidence.

Encourage Help

A person once told me, "Going it alone is for suckers." The better news is that you do not have to! When you're going to begin something new to you, gather your supporters. For example, I invite my graduate students who enroll in my public speaking class to gather a circle of friends. I suggest: "When you need to rehearse, you can rehearse the two–minute opening of a speech with one friend, the middle of the speech with another friend, and the ending with a third friend. You can even rehearse by calling a friend on your cell phone." I also invite the students to sign up for the Speaking Lab so that they can get more support, some coaching, and rehearsal time.

When you're gathering supporters, remember these two

distinctions:
a) Help them first.
b) Make it easy and fun for them to help you.

Some students balk at the idea of "Help them first." They ask, "How can I help someone?" I suggest, "You can contact them and ask, "How are things going?" And then you can listen to them. Listening is friendly and kind—and it's a supportive thing." Avoid merely calling upon people to ask them to do something for you. Be proactive. Call them just to connect and hear them out. They'll appreciate it. And some will even want to help you.

Finally, invest in yourself by hiring a coach or subject expert when you need help. For example, I've hired editors frequently; that's how I've written 21 previous books. Also, I hired two media coaches when I was preparing to launch a new product and to appear on radio and television. It's great to have multiple people watching my back.

"Feeling Comfortable" Is Not the Central Element of Confidence

Let's look at the above W.A.K.E. distinctions closely. You'll likely notice that "feeling comfortable" is *not* the central element. Instead, we're focused on preparing to adapt and getting support.

To act with confidence is to move forward despite fear. Your confidence does not arise from your knowing what is going to happen. Your confidence resides in your ability to adapt and learn all through the process. Over the years, I have faced fear many times—particularly when I have done something for the first time: giving my first speech to 697 people, directing my first feature film, recording my first audio program, writing my first book, and teaching my first college class. I was prepared for the fact that I would make mistakes, and I did make some. What helped was getting supporters, mentors, coaches, and editors.

Courage is easier when you're prepared.—Tom Marcoux

I prepared as best as I could. For example, I personally drew 805 storyboards for my first feature film. I knew the film backwards and forwards before I stepped onto the movie set.

Courage is the ability to act in the face of fear.—Phil Stutz

Commitment requires an endless series of small painful actions. —Phil Stutz and Barry Michels

Commit to preparation, and you can step forward with true confidence. And still, people want to feel better as they take courageous action. Hence, we'll now cover Methods to "Feel Confident."

Methods to "Feel Confident"

C – calm down through Heart Breathing
O – open your focus to "How are *You* doing?"
N – note "What would a confident person do?"
F – find things to be impressed about in the person
I – intensify an action
D – deep breathe before you speak
E – energize a good-pattern before under stress
N – notice and improve your posture
T – target "If you're afraid, rehearse"

1. Calm down through Heart Breathing
Place your hand over your heart. Breathe in through your nose. Hold the breath for a moment. Breathe out through your mouth. Some of my clients breathe in and say to themselves, "God relaxes me." Others focus on "I am relaxed." Choose what works for you. I invite you to practice this process every day—even for just 30 seconds. Soon you can just imagine doing this and immediately feel relaxed. For example, sometimes I recline on a seat on a train, and I can immediately relax.

2. Open your focus to "How are *You* Doing?"
When I was a shy nine-year-old playing the piano for seniors at a retirement home, I was terrified. My whole focus was on "How

am I doing?" and "Am I making a mistake?" Then, over years of giving speeches, I learned the power of switching to "How are YOU doing?"

The secret is to engage in the moment. Be right there with the person. This is also known as "being present." How do you do this? Watch the other person's face and body language. See how the person is responding and how you can be of service to him or her. When I give a speech, I watch faces and body language, and I modify my words to connect with my audience. Often, I'll ask a gentle question. By "gentle question," I mean a question that is easy for the person to answer and often is enjoyable for the person to answer.

In addition, I often introduce a topic with a question instead of a flat statement. Why? A statement invites resistance. Look at these two details:
a) Women live longer than men.
b) Why do women live longer than men?

Do you see how the question is intriguing?

Another Way to Get to "How are YOU Doing?"

At the beginning of a speech, I often ask: "When you first heard about my topic for today, what were you expecting and hoping that I would talk about?" Soon I'll ask, "What topic would really help you if I address it? I'll write down your questions and topics here [on a whiteboard]."

Do you see how I'm purposely engaging the audience and listening to them? I go on to say, "I'll address these questions as we go along. I do not do a canned speech. This is a real-time event." Often, a get a couple of chuckles with that statement.

I approach a speech with confidence because I'm not trying to impress people; my goal is to work with them and serve them.

3. Note "What would a confident person do?"

Ask yourself, "How would a confident person walk?" Also imagine how a confident person would stand. One of my clients pictured Sean Connery as James Bond, and my client would then walk with confidence and poise.

Here's another technique to use when meeting people at a networking event. Let's say three people are standing together talking. Hold a glass of water in one hand and smoothly walk up to them. Listen to the person talking. Take a drink of water, nod and smile at the people. When the speaker pauses, and the others turn toward you, ask a relevant question related to what the person was saying. Or you can simply say, "Hello, I'm [your name], and you are?" Most often, you'll be addressing the speaker, unless one of the listeners addresses you first.

Special Note: I suggest a glass of water because if someone jostles you, water is less troublesome than wine staining someone's clothes. Secondly, at a networking event, you want to be on your toes, and drinking alcohol may dull your senses a bit.

4. Find things to be impressed about in the person

Many people get nervous as they try to impress someone. That's a lot of work. Instead, change your focus and find things to be impressed about in the person you're talking with. Listen to what they emphasize. Find a sincere compliment to express. Here are examples:

- "Wow, you really held your cool in that situation."
- "That's a creative solution. I bet that was well received."
- "I appreciate how you led the group to a more helpful idea."

5. Intensify an action

My training as an actor gave me the paradigm of focusing on simple actions. For example, for some scenes, I could cry on cue simply by placing my hand over my heart.

To "intensify an action" is about focusing. Let's face it. Many of us at any given moment are scattered. Think of all the multi-tasking going on. Even as I write this I'm listening to music.

So how does one focus? Pick an objective. Objective is a word used often by actors. When the actor is clear on the character's objective (what he or she wants), the actor is focused. The actor's performance will radiate truth.

Further, to intensify an action, tie a simple action to your objective. What can the simple action be? Listening well, for example. Here are some examples of combining an action with an objective [objective in italics]:

- I'll listen well, and he'll feel good when talking with me.
- I'll smile, and she'll feel welcome at this networking event.

You can see the simple actions of listening and smiling culminating in a positive result for both you and your contact.

6. Deep breathe before you speak

My assistant said, "You always take a big breath before you start speaking to an audience." So this was a method that I did instinctively. By taking that big breath, my first sentence was always strong and confident. Why? Because I had enough breath support.

My training as an actor taught me to have enough breath (and oxygen) to support what I was saying.

Some people run out of breath in the middle of a sentence, especially when they're nervous at the beginning of a speech.

The truth is I have felt nervous at the beginning of a speech, but with a big breath before speaking, I did not appear nervous.

I watch my audience members' faces. I know that when I begin with a deep breath and a strong first sentence, the audience feels they are in good hands. I feel confident that I have begun well.

7. Energize a good–pattern before you're under stress

When I say "good–pattern," I'm talking about taking action in ways that build connection with the person or people you're talking with. But this requires preparation and practice.

I recommend putting your efforts into the good-pattern before you're under stress because people default to their conditioning when they're under stress (as noted in research studies). So you need to condition yourself to the good–pattern you want to exhibit. Here's another way of looking at it: "energize a good–pattern" means "choose excellent training."

I do not often refer to military principles, but this one is particularly useful in our current discussion: More sweat in training; less blood in battle.

Here are two Good–Patterns that you'll do well to prepare and practice:
a) *Gentle Questions*
These are questions that are easy–to–answer. They're positive in nature and invite conversation.

- "What's working for you at this conference?"
- "Which speaker are you looking forward to?"
- "What do you like about this association?"

b) *Reflective Replies*
When I say "Reflective Replies," I'm using the metaphor of a pool that reflects the image of a person. You function like a reflective pool as you assure the person that you're listening deeply and picking up what they're feeling.

- "That sounds frustrating."
- "That sounds painful. How did you keep going?"

To energize a good-pattern, first make a choice to train yourself or get training. Second, before you're in a stressful situation (like a job interview), rehearse. When you're in the stressful situation, use your training. Finally, after the stressful event, analyze how you did and adjust your subsequent rehearsal before the next time you face similar stressful conditions.

Excellent training and rehearsal fortify our feelings of confidence. We feel confident that we're as ready as we can be.

One last note: Choosing to train and rehearse is a keystone to personal freedom.

Your true freedom rests on your choice of your own programming.
—Tom Marcoux

8. Notice and improve your posture
Imagine that there is a string going through your spine and pulling up to the ceiling. And picture that all of your vertebrae line up. You are not arching your back. You are, instead, aligning your vertebrae. I learned from three physical therapists (during my recovery from a car accident) that when you align your vertebrae, you actually expend less energy than when you slouch. How is that possible? When you slouch, your muscles have to hold you up. But your back was designed to hold you up with ease—when your vertebrae are aligned.

In addition, when you hold yourself with good posture, you look strong, confident, and competent. And you feel better. Other people pick up this vibe from you. They treat you better, which reinforces your feelings of confidence.

9. Target "If you're afraid, rehearse"
When you really want to live on a more exciting and fulfilling level, you're going to be stretching and growing—and entering situations that are new to you.

For over a decade, I have coached clients and graduate/college students in the skills of excellent public speaking. They memorize a phrase: "If you're afraid, rehearse."

Think of it. If you're feeling nervous, you're already uncomfortable. Imagine putting that energy to work by rehearsing. I've rehearsed before job interviews and even before stepping up to meet a celebrity at an event. Whether I was to meet best–selling authors like Guy Kawasaki, Chip Conley, Debbie Ford and others . . . or entertainers/actors like Dionne Warwick and George Takei (of *Star Trek* fame), I rehearsed. After all, it would do me no good to get tongue–tied when I met them. Instead, I knew ahead of time what I wanted to say concisely, and I was sure that I had chosen words that I could easily express.

Why rehearse? To create a New Choice Conditioned Response, which is your desired action in a given situation. The process includes the following steps:
a) you make a deliberate choice to create a new behavior.
b) you rehearse the desired behavior.
c) under a stressful or at least critical situation, you implement the desired behavior.

In other words: **You make a Cool Decision before a Hot Event.**

I describe this as: you make a careful choice of behavior before you experience the stressful situation.

I learned the value of creating my own *New Choice Conditioned Response* when I studied acting and had to learn numerous lines for a play. I came up with my own method. I recorded the play using different voices (impersonating other actors), and then I left empty spaces so that I would be able to respond with my lines. In essence, the other actors' lines served as "triggers" for my responding line of dialogue. In essence, I conditioned (trained) myself to respond to the trigger–lines of dialogue with my lines spoken by the character I was portraying.

Rehearsal, to me, is part of a process I call the Trigger–Set Method that I first introduced in my book *Nothing Can Stop You This Year!*

To feel confident, it often helps to identify triggers that will be present in the stressful environment that you will enter. Then you identify how you can train yourself (condition yourself) to take effective action.

Earlier I talked about how I take a deep breath before I say my first line of a speech. That's my own New Choice Conditioned Response. It supports my coming across as confident and competent.

The Trigger–Set Method in Brief:

1. Identify a trigger to be present at the stressful event
2. Choose an empowering action.
3. Associate that empowering action with the trigger and rehearse that empowering action.
4. Implement that empowering action.

In addition, you can create your own positive trigger. For example, during a speech, a speaker can hold a Post–it note with her thumb and forefinger. This Post–it Note includes key words to serve as an outline for the speech. Holding that Post–it Note reassures her that she has something to fall back on if needed. This boosts her feelings of confidence.

Points to Remember:

P.I.E. for Confidence

Principle: Drop the idea that you need to feel comfortable to act like a confident person.

Inquiry: What would help you feel like you can adapt to whatever may come up in the stressful situation? How will you implement the methods for feeling confident?

Emotional Strength: The essence of transformation is consistent rehearsal and creating your New Choice Conditioned Response.

What do you intend to use to strengthen your "feeling confident"?

Will you do some of the following?
a) Heart Breathing
b) Focus on "How are you doing?"
c) Identify "What would a confident person do?"
d) Find things to be impressed about in the person
e) Deep breathe before you speak
f) Energize a good–pattern before you're under stress
g) Improve your posture

h) Use the process, "If you're afraid, rehearse"

(The above is an excerpt from *Create Your Best Life: Unleash Your Charisma and Confidence to Change the World.*)

3. HOW DO YOU HANDLE FEAR?

How do you deal with fear when it comes up? Let's focus on this statement:

Our fears must never hold us back from pursuing our hopes.
—John F. Kennedy

I developed a process for dealing with my fears. I don't deny my fears. I use my fears as signals for more preparation. Courage is easier when you're prepared.

For example, if I feel jitters before an appearance on television or radio, I rehearse possible questions and my responses that I pose in the form of sound bites.

How Can You Get Yourself to Take Risks?

Become strategic in how you approach risks. It is important to take appropriate risks. You need to set reasonable criteria for excellence. To set reasonable criteria when strategizing on a goal, use the R.E.A.C.H. process:

R–Reduce risk
E–Expect results
A–Adjust to circumstances

C–Compensate for your own shortcomings
H–Hook your attention

Reduce Risk

When you are working toward a goal, especially one that will change your life, huge fears are likely to loom in front of you. Many of them are unreal, although they will paralyze you if you let them. Risks that are created within your own mind cannot be overcome. But others will be quite real, and you will have to face them. Your task is to identify which risks are likely to pop up and which ones are being generated by fear gone wild.

For instance, Tara is a stay–at–home mom who wants to go back to school so she can apply for a top–level job. The problem is she must deal with childcare issues. Who can she trust with her child? What can go wrong?

The real challenge is finding responsible daycare that can accommodate her needs. But if Tara's mind races ahead, she might become fearful that putting her little darling in childcare will ruin his life and that he'll start stealing hubcaps when he's thirteen because his mother abandoned him. Tara needs to pause and consider that no daycare center can reduce that imagined risk.

Like Tara, we cannot control the distant future. You can only face what is in front of you right now. The best way to do that is to identify what will likely go wrong and then create a plan to reduce the chances that it will.

On the other hand, letting fear run out of control will not only distract you from important tasks, but, at its worst, it will shut you down. It is almost impossible to have a sense of adventure and to be creative when you're locked in fear. Thus, whenever you reduce unnecessary fear, you open yourself to creativity. And ultimately, you reduce unnecessary risks because you head trouble off at the pass.

At this first stage, think ahead to what you are likely to encounter when you execute your plan. What snafus could arise? What challenges lie ahead? Sometimes it helps to ask friends to brainstorm with you possible scenarios you might need to prepare for.

Now identify the problems you can actually prepare for and begin to form a strategy. When people do this, they immediately feel stronger because they feel more in control of their own destiny. My clients protect their jobs by maintaining a job diary; they log their successes for composing a summary page for their annual performance review. What I have just described is the core of preparation, and it will greatly improve your chances for success.

Expect Results

You have identified what can go wrong and developed some ideas for avoiding adverse consequences. Now it is time to focus on the kind of results you expect. Specific results. It's not good enough to say, "I want to be a happier person," or "I want to find love in my life," or "I want to reduce stress so I can just relax." Admirable goals, certainly, but they're too vague.

You need to identify precisely the results you hope to achieve. What do they look like? What benefits will they bring you? How will you feel better when the results occur? Asking yourself these questions will help you tailor your plan toward the right destination, which will keep you on track.

Keep in mind that you are not the only person who will be affected by this goal. Your life touches so many others. The benefits of your success may affect your mate, children, extended family, friends, co–workers or your clients or customers. I call these people your "stakeholders" because they have a stake in the outcome of your goals. Consequently, you need to also consider the expectations of others.

Others peoples' expectations are likely to be different from your own. For instance, if you are contemplating a change in careers, your only concern could be that the new career is more satisfying and interesting than your current one. Your spouse's concern, however, could be that you bring in a higher salary. It is important to communicate your plans to those who will be most affected, and to make sure you are all on the same page.

Find out your spouse's expectations and priorities. Whose satisfaction matters the most? If you are married, you have to consider your mate first. But what about customers? If you change a product or service, will you lose your client base?

Consider interviewing those who will be impacted by your plan. Conduct surveys among your stakeholders to determine what priorities and results are important to them.

Adjust to Circumstances

Now that you know your risks and expectations, you need to evaluate your life circumstances. Are you in a position to go after your goal or do you have to adjust either the goal or your life? Right now you are only in the strategy stage, so you're not making adjustments for anything that is actually happening to you. You are sitting down and playing out your future in your own mind.

What position are you in financially, domestically, socially and with your career? What constraints are on you? Now consider the demands that your goal will place on your life. What challenges will it throw your way? Try to picture the changes in your life when you're asked to devote more money, time or effort. What adjustments will you have to consider in order to make your plan work?

Nothing is free. If we don't pay for it with money, we pay for it with our time, energy or health.—Carmen Renee Berry

Carmen's quote means that when you set a goal for yourself, you have to understand that it's going to cost you something. Years ago I was the sole proprietor of my own company. I knew before I ever started that family members might need me during tough times, and that I would have to be there for them. I was prepared to care for my sweetheart when she fell ill. I was able to hire a friend to help out.

An important part of your strategy is to identify what aspects you can drop when necessary. These droppables are significant because the enthusiasm that comes from the planning process sometimes makes us blind to our life's inevitable limitations. We may not have the time or resources for everything. So know ahead of time what the keepers are and what can be let go.

A man is rich in proportion to the number of things he can afford to let alone.—Henry David Thoreau

My client Maggie wanted to be a full-time professional speaker. She researched the career and found that she had to provide speaker products: books, audio programs and so on. At first she planned on making a first-rate audio program with a music soundtrack. Once she evaluated the situation, she decided that original background music was an expensive addition and was droppable. Though a year later, when Maggie was pulling in one speaking engagement after another, she made a second edition of her program and added music to it.

Sharon, a realtor, planned to create full color brochures but the recession slowed her business to a trickle. She adjusted her approach to include much more in–person networking and relied on her business card, personal warmth and sending out e–newsletters.

Nedra, the founder of a non-profit organization, shifted her plans and started blogging and linking to other blogs. Her strategy was to increase her efforts with social networking in ways that involved her energy but not using up funds.

Compensate for Your Own Shortcomings

As you pictured this project in your mind, you have imagined all the things that could possibly go wrong "out there." But what about you? What about your own personal shortcomings—the qualities or liabilities that could hold you back? It is time to look inward. You stand a much better chance of crossing the finish line if you aren't grandiose about your own capacities, and if you can realistically assess what you're capable of.

Identify your tendencies or shortcomings now in the planning stage, and then figure out how to compensate for them. For example, I am a fast-moving person. When I edit my own films, I naturally create quick cuts, which is a sequence of images of short duration. I know that I have this general tendency in whatever I do, which can work against me. This is why I always have two people with me in the editing room who will continually offer their opinion on the output. Remember this phrase:

Know your tendencies and compensate for them.—Tom Marcoux

One tendency can prevent success: Letting fear of rejection cause a dead stop to your efforts.

Being rejected doesn't hold you back from anything. Only YOU hold yourself back. If you are told no, ask for what you'd have to do to get it, or ask again at another time when the circumstances have changed. Ask if they know someone else who might say yes. When you realize that there's no merit to rejection, you'll feel more comfortable asking for things. But you may need a bit of help learning how to ask for what you want.—Jack Canfield

Every top achiever I have interviewed has demonstrated the power to persist through rejection. As I mentioned earlier, the bestselling series of books, *Chicken Soup for the Soul* (over 100 million sold), was rejected by publishers 141 times. It only took one publisher to team up with the authors to make their first book a success.

To successfully deal with rejection, make your reason to do something so huge that you'll push past any hesitation. One of my secrets is to have a team of consultants assist me with my projects. This ensures that my work is of top caliber and will truly serve the intended audience.

Hook Your Attention

How can you inspire yourself? You need to find out what it is about your goal that really grabs you. Your inspiration will allow you to stick with it even when your energy sags. You are about to invest a great deal of time, energy and money in the pursuit of your goal. You might even be asking loved ones to do the same and take a stake in your future. Find the heart of your passion, the fire that will keep burning no matter what failure and heartaches might come. And you have to do this before you take a single step on the path.

In the early sixties, President John F. Kennedy said these words:

I believe that this nation should commit itself to achieving the goal, before this decade is out, of landing a man on the moon and returning him safely to the earth.—John F. Kennedy

Let's realize that there was no space program to speak of when Kennedy made this statement. He was envisioning something that didn't exist, and he committed to it simply because he believed in it. Those few choice words mobilized a nation and gave it hope. It was a catchphrase that had great power. You need a catchphrase or a hook that does the same for you: one that inspires a belief in yourself and in your future. A hook, by its very nature, is short and to the point. My own mission caption for my coaching/speaking work is:

I help people experience enthusiasm, love, and wisdom to fulfill big dreams.

The mainstay of hook your attention is to zero–in on your unique essence. To create a life of fulfillment, you must be different from the average person. You need to have an extraordinary focus.

The problems of the world cannot possibly be solved by skeptics or cynics whose horizons are limited by the obvious realities. We need [people] who can dream of things that never were.—John F. Kennedy

Another example of a hook is Roy O. Disney's statement:

Decision making is easy when your values are clear.—Roy O. Disney

As the brother and business partner of Walt Disney, Roy knew that whatever new ventures the Disney Company went into (after Walt's death), they wouldn't go wrong if they stuck to the company's established values.

Make your hook short, simple, and articulate. Make sure it encapsulates the heart and soul of your goal. When you repeat it to yourself, make sure it brings up powerful emotions and gives you a strong sense of direction.

We create encouraging, energizing edutainment for our good and humankind's rise.—Mission Caption of Tom Marcoux Media, LLC

Your hook or catchphrase will help you connect emotionally with the essence of your goal every time you say it.

Write two versions of your personal catchphrase into your personal journal.

4. HOW DO YOU KEEP GOING DESPITE DISAPPOINTMENT AND FRUSTRATION?

Support Yourself

What can you do if you're hit with a surprising loss?
Pause. Pay attention.

Loss saps our energy. It can make us go into a state of shock. We need time to grieve and function.

Often, we do not have the energy to implement helpful suggestions. In fact, we may find ourselves resisting good ideas, and saying, "No. That won't work." A loss can plunge us into negative thinking.

Courage consists in the power of self–recovery.—Ralph Waldo Emerson

During a crisis, you need courage to act. Also, you need the strength to restrain yourself from harmful, rash decisions. For example, I know a family in which one parent lost a job. The family posted an ad on the Internet to sell a car and received 12 inquiries for it. Unfortunately, they went with the second offer. They did not have the courage to hold out for a better price.

Where do we get such strength?

A first step is to make time to grieve. We need this time. Morrie Schwartz was slowly dying from ALS. His body was shutting down, requiring a nurse and family members to take care of his bodily functions. His friend and former student Mitch Albom chronicled Morrie's journey in *Tuesdays with Morrie*. Morrie said, "There are some mornings when I cry and cry and mourn for myself. Some mornings, I'm so angry and bitter. But it doesn't last too long. Then I get up and say, 'I want to live.'"

My clients often find it helpful to release their emotions in a personal journal. If the emotions and thoughts bother you so much, you can rip out the page and burn it so that no one (including you) can ever read it.

People are not aware that it is often empathy they are needing.—Marshall B. Rosenberg

The central idea of supporting yourself is to give yourself the empathy that you need.

We must learn what will truly soothe ourselves. Let's face it.

Some losses can feel even more shocking and painful because they arrive as bad surprises. I once lost a dear friend who committed suicide. Up to that moment, I had never felt deep grief. Following his death, I needed empathy; I needed to hear myself. So I supported myself by writing in my personal journal.

In an economic recession, people are slammed with loss from every side. People lose their jobs, retirement funds, set career paths, homes and more. These people can express empathy and kindness to themselves in the form of a *Low Mood First Aid Kit*. This kit is actually a list of activities you can do to nurture yourself.

Here is a secret from John F. Kennedy:

Leadership and learning are indispensable to each other.
—John F. Kennedy

So learn to take action to soothe yourself. My clients have included these items in their Low Mood First Aid Kit:

- Quiet time with an uplifting book (to help you learn of new possibilities)
- Music
- Prayer
- Meditation
- Writing in a personal journal
- Dancing to a favorite song in my room
- Walking in nature
- Exercise
- Time with a pet
- Belly breathing

Belly breathing is an important tool to bring your focus back to yourself. To do this, breathe in through your nose and allow your belly to inflate to its fullest. Briefly hold in your breath, and then breathe out while your belly deflates. I've heard my audience members comment how this process releases stress from their shoulders, and that they felt calm and even hopeful. I invite you to include belly breathing in your Low Mood First Aid Kit.

Where the spirit does not work with the hand, there is no art.—Leonardo da Vinci

You reconnect your spirit to your life when you demonstrate empathy and compassion for yourself. Remember that a sudden loss can put many of us into an emotional shutdown. We must learn to ride out a crisis with bravery and grace, and then nurture ourselves so that we can, in essence, create art out of our lives. Adding in time for meditation or prayer will help make this part of your personal path.

A hero is an ordinary individual who finds the strength to persevere and endure in spite of overwhelming obstacles.—Christopher Reeve

Paralyzed and confined to his wheelchair for nine years, Christopher Reeve found a new purpose in speaking up for people suffering with spinal chord injuries. He directed two films from that chair. Chris even coached his son on how to ride a bicycle with his words alone. Christopher Reeve, who was famous for playing Superman, had become a hero in real life.

We learn that heroes take care of themselves so that they can think clearly and do what needs to be done.

All our knowledge has its origins in our perceptions.
—Leonardo da Vinci

Da Vinci's comment wakes us up to an important point. People who don't take care of themselves are easily susceptible to having false and skewed perceptions. This section helps you take care of yourself physically and emotionally.

The truth no one will tell you: Too much of what the media and society tell us is completely built on false and skewed perceptions.

If you want to be rich, you cannot be normal.—Noah St. John

Also, if you want to be happy, even during an economic crisis, you cannot be normal. You must take extraordinary care of yourself. And you need access to your inner wisdom.

A Powerful Way to Access Your Inner Wisdom

A secret from Mozart guides us in gaining access to our own wisdom and even inspiration from Higher Power.

When I am traveling in a carriage, or walking after a good meal, or during the night when I cannot sleep; it is on such occasions that ideas flow best and most abundantly.—Wolfgang Amadeus Mozart

Mozart's comment reminds us about timing and making space to access our inner wisdom. My clients have pen and paper near their bed and in their pocket or purse to write down helpful ideas whenever they arise. Such helpful ideas can be about how to reach out to customers or how to schedule some downtime away from your business or family members (like having one's sister take the kids on Thursday evenings). This process will help you to feel hopeful, and better able to start to turn things in your favor.

Energy and persistence conquer all things.—Benjamin Franklin

In order to persist, you need to support yourself by finding ways to consistently replenish your energy. One of my clients has a list that includes books, music, DVDs (for example, a TV show with no commercials) and humor-filled shows like "Who's Line is it Anyway?"

Be sure to write a list of ways to support yourself. When you take action, you'll have the energy you need to persist.

The Three Elements of Supporting Yourself

The truth no one will tell you: You need three things to truly support yourself during the bumpiness of daily life:

1. Take care of yourself
2. Grieve
3. Regain energy

An economic crisis brings loss. The best way I can express this is to share a personal example. When my dear friend (close, like a brother) committed suicide, for the first time I was plunged into deep grief. I hadn't known what grief was before then.

In deep pain, I applied the three elements. I took care of myself by slowing down my schedule. I also told my graduate students the truth: "My friend has died, so I may lose my voice for thirty seconds. But that's okay. We'll flow forward." In this way, when grief surprised me and choked me up, I allowed it to have a place. I also wrote about it in my personal journal.

I did gentle things to guard my energy. I replied to a number of e-mails with: "Please feel comfortable to follow–up with me in two weeks." I continued to exercise and eat nutritious food. I even watched DVDs of favorite shows to give myself brief vacations from thinking of my grief.

Please write in your personal journal how you can: take care of yourself, grieve and regain energy.

Principle:
When hit with a bad surprise, be sure to grieve and to regain energy.

Power Question:
How can you take care of yourself, grieve and regain your energy?

5. HOW CAN YOU MAKE SURE TO HAVE PERSONAL ENERGY TO EXCEL?

Act then Recover

To resolve a roadblock to success of no personal energy, you need to become skillful about replenishing your energy. To do this, learn the *Activity–Recovery Pattern*. First, identify your prime time. For me, a great time for writing is when I first get up in the morning. I am refreshed and excited by the new day.

Second, make sure to tackle your important tasks during your prime time. Perhaps your prime time is in the afternoon when you are most alert. If so, schedule your crucial team meetings to fall during that time frame. If you need to devote prime time to writing a report, make an appointment with yourself. Place your cell phone into take–a–message mode.

Third, identify elements for your Low Mood First Aid Kit (which we discussed earlier). Your Low Mood First Aid Kit is a list of things you can do to raise your tone and energy level. Perhaps you will benefit from a walk, a brief phone call with a loved one or energizing music.

When I need to energize myself, I step aboard my exercise machine and call a close friend. It feels great to take care of my body, and my soul feels enriched, too.

Fourth, honor your natural rhythms. For example, my client Mary is a writer. She will write for one hour and then "it just doesn't feel like fun anymore." At that point, she will take a break. In college, I studied for 50 minutes and then took a ten–minute break to step outside and walk around the library building. In this way I could study for 12 hours a day.

It is crucial to get in recovery time every day. When you have enough rest, you will have a reservoir of patience. For example, one year I was teaching a particular online class. I witnessed a student making mean remarks about another student's posted comments. In reply, I wrote the following comment. I am glad that I had programmed in recovery time so I had the energy to write this message.

Hello,
This concerns the comment that upset Sophie. [I quoted a student who expressed her upset about an insult that was posted about her own posted thoughts.] This inspires deep sadness in me. Let's go gently here in this discussion area. Let's simply state an idea and leave it at that. Let's not push vigorously against anyone, any particular group or any particular idea. This posting board does not give us a chance to provide a comment in a gentle voice. So let's be gentle with our words. Thank you all. Tom

It was important that I write a message that showed the path of light and compassion. I also avoided chastising the errant student.

To my relief, the troublemaker sent me an e–mail with the words, "I apologize."

Making sure that I had recovery time enabled me to underreact, or rather, respond to the situation with compassion and quiet strength.

Devote time to recreation. This is better than a one–for–one benefit. I have noticed that when I have some rest and recreation, I return to work with three times the efficiency and effectiveness. It's worth it!

6. HOW CAN YOU OVERCOME PROCRASTINATION AND MAKE SIGNIFICANT PROGRESS?

Measure Progress

To resolve a roadblock to success of no personal discipline (to overcome procrastination), you need a strategic plan and a means to measure your progress. Researchers point out that procrastination is actually about anticipated pain. The truth is that we need a big enough why so that we will flow through anticipated pain. We need to set powerful goals.

We also need to make taking action (for our goals) into a game that we can win. When we vividly feel our progress, we create a good feeling that allows us to set aside the anticipated pain that fosters procrastination. *Keep Score and Achieve More.* That is, set up simple ways to achieve milestones. These milestones will provide you with energy and motivation. For example, when I write a book, I keep a log of how many words I write per day. A salesperson can keep a log of how many sales phone calls and closed sales she achieves.

To create a viable game, we need to set up appropriate measurements.

If you can't measure it, you can't manage it.—Ken Blanchard

Measurement is the first step that leads to control and eventually to improvement. If you can't measure something, you can't understand it. If you can't understand it, you can't control it. If you can't control it, you can't improve it.—H. James Harrington

Ken Blanchard has a story that illustrates the value of incremental measurement.

How do they train killer whales to jump over the rope at Sea World? Do they hang a rope 20 feet over the pool and then shout to the whale 'Up, up, up!' No. They start with the rope under the water. When the whale swims over the rope, it gets rewarded. Then the rope is gradually raised. Each time the whale swims over it, again, a reward is given. How often do you give a 'reward' to those with whom you work? Only when the final goal is reached or do you give praise along the way as incremental progress is made?—Ken Blanchard

A powerful way to measure progress is to use a *Self–Leadership Chart* in which you note activities you want to do on a daily basis. For example, my client Stephanie lists these daily activities:

- Write for 20 minutes in the morning before going to work
- Write for 20 minutes during my lunch hour
- Take a 20 minute walk during my lunch hour
- Take a 20 minute walk with my spouse after work

Be sure to check the chart every day. This will keep the important tasks in your mind.

Principle:
To make significant progress, set up appropriate steps for incremental measurement.

Power Questions:
How can you measure your progress? What can you place in a Self–Leadership Chart to ensure that you make daily progress?

7. WHAT IS THE ESSENCE OF ENHANCING BUSINESS AND PERSONAL RELATIONSHIPS?

Enhance Relationships

Have you lost a job or is your business slowing down during a recession? What's the solution? Relationships.

A number of people feel cast adrift at sea, and they feel uncomfortable in networking or asking favors of people they know.

What can you do? Let's look at the essence of a healthy relationship. It's a place you go to give, create connection and later to receive. I tell my graduate students: "**The Magic 3 Words of Networking** are *help them first*."

Many details that work for a good friendship also work for a good professional relationship.

First, people want to know that you care. And they want to feel important. When you help your supervisor look good to her boss, you are building your relationship with your supervisor.

To improve your relationship:
a) accept feelings
b) keep agreements
c) turn complaints into action or a request and
d) tell the truth.—Gay Hendricks

When networking, the idea is make a small promise to someone when you meet the person. As you listen carefully to a new person, find some kind action you can do on her behalf. If she mentions a hobby or an interest of her son or daughter, make a promise to send a link to a web site (if possible). Follow through on such a promise that same day. This is a process of keeping your agreements.

I often say, "How can I be supportive of what you're doing?" Then I listen carefully.

To build stronger friendships, let's remember:

To love a person is to learn the song that's in their heart, and to sing it to them when they have forgotten.—Thomas Chandler

Remember to build relationships, you need to listen well, make appropriate promises, keep agreements and truly look out for the well–being of people in your circle. A simple important process is to call up people and catch up with their lives. Pay attention. People have a deep craving to feel important. Provide your attention and you'll be a welcome part of their lives. Give your attention first and later some people in your circle will be glad to help you with job leads and other supportive activities.

(The above material for Topics 3–7 is from *Truth No One Will Tell You*.)

A FINAL WORD AND SPRINGBOARD TO YOUR SUCCESS

Congratulations on your efforts with this book.

We have covered ***countermeasures*** to the Darkest Secrets of Making a Pitch for Film and Television:

- *Darkest Secret #1: It's not what you claim, but what you show that counts.*
- *Darkest Secret #2: "Neediness" gives off a smell—and it stinks.*
- *Darkest Secret #3: Confidence attracts, arrogance repels.*
- *Darkest Secret #4: Grab their attention or crash and burn.*
- *Darkest Secret #5: People decide quickly, based on little information.*
- *Darkest Secret #6: Show fear and you're fried.*
- *Darkest Secret #7: Some people will try to make you fail.*

Then we explored 18 sections that expanded your skills for giving the best pitch that you can.

To gain more value from this book, be sure to go through it and develop your own To Do List. Take some action. Any action towards improving skills and promoting yourself is helpful. I often say, "Better than zero."

The best to you and may your dreams come true,

Tom

Tom Marcoux
Motion Picture Producer, Director, Screenwriter, Actor

P.S. In terms of this section being a springboard to your dreams, I invite you to return to these pages and practice the various methods so that you continue to become stronger.

For more training, please consider my other books in this series:

- *Darkest Secrets of Film Directing: How Successful Film Directors Overcome Hidden Traps*

- *Darkest Secrets of the Film and Television Industry Every Actor Should Know: A Film Director and Actor Reveals Secrets of Acting, Auditions, Movie Roles and Self–Promotion*

- *Darkest Secrets of Persuasion and Seduction Masters: How to Protect Yourself and Turn the Power to Good*

- *Darkest Secrets of Negotiation Masters: How to Protect Yourself, Overcome Intimidation, Get Stronger and Turn the Power to Good*

Two other books are especially helpful to people seeking to pitch well and get their films and screenplays produced:

- *Be Heard and Be Trusted, 3rd edition*

- *Nothing Can Stop You This Year!, 2nd edition*

Gain special training through a subscription service (including (all books available through Amazon.com and BN.com [BarnesandNoble.com])

Gain special training through my *Top Five Group Elite Video Training* (for information go to YouTube.com and type in "Tom Marcoux Top Five Group").

Consider my workshops and presentations and view free articles at my blog: www.BeHeardandBeTrusted.com

Contact: tomsupercoach@gmail.com

EXCERPT

From
Darkest Secrets of Persuasion and Seduction Masters: How to Protect Yourself and Turn the Power to Good
by Tom Marcoux

. . . Now, I am in my 40's, with gray in my hair, and for 27 years I have been taking action to protect people.

And now is the time for me to protect you with the Countermeasures I reveal in this book.

Every human being needs to be able to
break the trance that a Manipulator
creates. You need to make good decisions
so you are safe and you keep growing
—and you are not cut down and crippled.

This Darkest Secrets material is so intense that I first released it only with the counterbalance of my most energizing and uplifting books, *Nothing Can Stop You This Year! and 10 Seconds to Wealth: Master the Moment Using Your Divine Gifts.*

An interviewer asked me: "Who can be the Manipulator?"
A co-worker, a boss, a salesperson, someone you're dating, and someone you think is a friend.

Now is the time—this very minute—for me to write this book to protect you.

I must speak the truth.

These darkest secrets of "persuasion masters" are …

Wait a minute! Let's say it plainly: These are the darkest secrets of masters of manipulation. Throughout this book, I will call these people what they are: Manipulators.

Dictionary.com defines "manipulate" as "To influence or manage shrewdly or deviously.… To tamper with or falsify for personal gain."

In this book, we will look on a manipulator as one who deviously influences someone with no concern about that person's well-being, and who causes harm to that person.

Here is the first Darkest Secret:

Darkest Secret #1:
Manipulators Make You Hurt
and Then Offer the Salve.

Manipulators would invite you to go out in the sun for hours and then sell you the salve to soothe your burns. The problem is that we don't notice that this is what they're doing.

For example, you're considering the purchase of a house. A Manipulator asks the question, "So, where would you put your TV?" This question is designed to put you into a trance.

Dictionary.com defines "trance" as "a half–conscious state,

seemingly between sleeping and waking, in which ability to function voluntarily may be suspended." Let's condense this: in a trance you may not be able to function freely.

Here is the second Darkest Secret:

**Darkest Secret #2:
Manipulators Put You into a Trance.**

To protect yourself, you must learn to use Countermeasures to Break the Trance. All the Countermeasures (actions you can take to break the trance) in this book will make you stronger and more capable of protecting yourself.

Now, we'll view the third Darkest Secret:

**Darkest Secret #3:
Manipulators Care Nothing for You and Human Decency: They'll lie, cheat, and do whatever they need to do so they win —but their charm masks all this.**

Let's return to the example of a Manipulator selling you a house. A Manipulator does not pause for an instant to see if you can truly afford the new house. The Manipulator would neglect to mention that you will not only have your mortgage payment of $900. There will be additional costs: home repairs, property tax, water, electricity, homeowner's insurance, and more. The Manipulator only emphasizes what he or she knows you want to hear: "Look! $900 is better than the $1500 you're paying for rent, which is just going down the toilet. And the $900 is an investment."

Let's go back to Darkest Secret #1:
Manipulators make you hurt and then offer the salve.

The Manipulator has you feeling good about the solution (salve) and feeling bad about your current life situation.

How? A Manipulator will make you hurt through questions such as:

- What bothers you about paying $1500 a month for rent? (The Manipulator will use a derisive tone when he says the word rent.)
- What is not smart about paying rent on someone else's house instead of investing in your own house?
- How do you feel about your children walking in the neighborhood where you live now?

Do you see how these questions are designed to make you hurt enough so that you'll buy?

An interviewer asked me, "Tom, aren't these good arguments for purchasing a house?"

"What we're looking at is the *intention* of the influencer," I replied. "Let's look at our definition of a manipulator as one who deviously influences someone with no concern about that person's well–being, and who causes harm to that person. If the person truly cannot afford the house, he or she will be harmed by buying it. If the manipulator conceals the truth, the manipulator is doing harm. That's the important difference."

Some friends of mine are ethical and helpful real estate agents who truthfully reveal the whole situation and help the purchaser achieve her own goals.

In this book, we are talking about another type of person; that is, unethical Manipulators.

* * *

In any given moment, we need to remember the tactics Manipulators use. We will focus on the word D.A.R.K. so you can remember details easily and protect yourself from Manipulators.

D—Dangle something for nothing
A—Alert to scarcity

R—Reveal the Desperate Hot Button
K—Keep on pushing buttons

1. Dangle Something for Nothing

What do conmen and conwomen do to seize your attention? They make you think you're getting a "steal."

I recently saw a documentary in which a conman on a street in England showed a toy that looked like it was dancing. This fake product was actually dancing because of a hidden, invisible thread. The conman was dangling something for nothing. The Entranced Buyer thought he was getting something worth $20 for only $5. That was the trick. The Entranced Buyer felt that he was getting $15 extra of value for his $5. What the Buyer really got was something worth nothing. Similarly, I know someone who purchased a copy of a Disney movie from a street vendor in San Francisco. She brought the copy home and it was unwatchable—and the street vendor was never seen again.

An old phrase goes, "A conman cannot con someone who is not looking for something for nothing."

How to Protect Yourself from "Dangle Something for Nothing"

Stop! Get on your cell phone and talk through the "deal" with someone you know who thinks clearly. Go home. Think about it. Do some research on the Internet. Listen to your gut feelings. If the salesman or conman is too insistent, get away from that Manipulator. Get quiet. Have a cup of water. Cool down. Break the Trance!

Break the Trance and Identify the Crucial Detail

Earlier, I mentioned that a Manipulator puts you into a trance. An added problem is that we put ourselves into a trance. For example, as you read this, are you thinking about your right toe? Most likely not (unless you stubbed your toe recently).

The point is that we only focus on a tiny percentage of what is going on in our life.

Around fifteen years ago, I caused myself trouble because I put myself into a trance. I discovered that under certain conditions, friendship can make you nearly deaf. Here's how: I was producing a song for a motion picture. A good friend was singing backup in the chorus. Because of our friendship, I wanted him to sound great. I completely missed the Crucial Detail. In this kind of situation, the Crucial Detail is that what truly counts is how the lead singer sounds! I made a song that I could not release. What a waste of time and money! I had put myself into a trance.

In any situation in which the Manipulator is "dangling something for nothing," we often fall into a trance and miss the Crucial Detail. The most important detail is not that we're saving money if we order before midnight tonight. What counts is whether the product creates a lasting, crucial benefit in our lives. And is the benefit of the product worth the cost? Some people even program themselves to make mistakes by saying, "I can't pass up a bargain." The bargain is *not* the Crucial Detail.

Secrets to Break the Trance

This is the process of B.R.E.A.K.S. It will help you remember the proven methods to break a trance.

B—Breathe
R—Relax
E—Envision
A—Act on aromas
K—Keep moving
S—Smile

Secret #1: Breathe
Remember *Darkest Secret #1: Manipulators make you hurt and then offer the salve.* The Manipulator wants to put you into a state of being that fills you with a sense of urgency and anxiety. *Oh, no! I'm going to miss the sale!*

Stop this highly vulnerable state. Take a deep breath. Do it now. Take a deep breath and let your belly "get fat" by filling it with air. As you breathe out, let your belly deflate. Breathe in through your nose and breathe out through your mouth. This is called *belly–breathing*. Repeat the actions of belly–breathing three times. Good. Now, do you feel different? Remember, when you are relaxed, you are strong.

End of Excerpt from *Darkest Secrets of Persuasion and Seduction Masters: How to Protect Yourself and Turn the Power to Good*

Available at Amazon.com and BN.com (BarnesandNoble.com)

ABOUT THE AUTHOR
TOM MARCOUX

Tom Marcoux helps people like you fulfill big dreams. Winner of a special award at the Emmys, Tom wrote, directed, and produced a feature film that went to the Cannes film market, where it gained international distribution.

As America's Communication Coach and TFG* Thought Leader, Tom has authored 22 books with sales in 15 countries. One of his books rose to **#1 on Amazon.com Hot New Releases**.

Tom and his team focus on his graphic novel/feature film series:

- *Jack AngelSword* (fantasy–thriller)—see video on YouTube: type in "Jack AngelSword Mayan Ruin")
- *Crystal Pegasus* (children's fantasy)—graphic novel available on Amazon.com
- *TimePulse* (science–fiction)—see www.facebook.com/timepulsegraphicnovel

Tom is also the author of two other film/TV industry–related books:

- *Darkest Secrets of Film Directing: How Successful Film Directors Overcome Hidden Traps*

- *Darkest Secrets of the Film and Television Industry Every Actor Should Know: A Film Director and Actor Reveals Secrets for Your Acting, Auditions, Movie Roles and Self–Promotion*

Tom also guides clients and audiences (IBM, Sun Microsystems) to success in job interviewing, public speaking, media relations, and branding. As a member of the National Speakers Association, he is a coach and guest expert on TV, radio, and print, and was dubbed "the Personal Branding Instructor" by the *San Francisco Examiner.* Tom addressed six National Association of Broadcasters' Conferences.

With a degree in psychology, Tom is a guest lecturer at Stanford University and California State University, and teaches public speaking, business communication and comparative religion at Academy of Art University. Using Tom's public speaking methods, one of his graduate students won the Charles Schwab Scholarship.

Visit TomSuperCoach.com and
Tom's blog at www.BeHeardandBeTrusted.com.
Visit: http://www.facebook.com/tom.marcoux.5
Contact Tom Marcoux at tomsupercoach@gmail.com

* TFG–*Top Five Group*

OTHER BOOKS BY TOM MARCOUX

Excel in the Film and Television Industry:

- *Darkest Secrets of Film Directing: How Successful Film Directors Overcome Hidden Traps*
- *Darkest Secrets of the Film and Television Industry Every Actor Should Know: A Film Director and Actor Reveals Secrets for Your Acting, Auditions, Movie Roles and Self–Promotion*

Use Top Communication Skills for Your Success:

- *Be Heard and Be Trusted: How You Can Use Secrets of the Greatest Communicators to Get What You Want*
- *Darkest Secrets of Charisma: Overcome the Lies about Personal Magnetism, Get People to Feel Your Charisma and Influence Others with Your Words*
- *Darkest Secrets of Persuasion and Seduction Masters: How to Protect Yourself and Turn the Power to Good*
- *Darkest Secrets of Negotiation Masters: How to Protect Yourself, Overcome Intimidation, Get Stronger and Turn the Power to Good*
- *Secrets of Awesome Dinner Guests: What Walt Disney, Steve Jobs, Oprah Winfrey, Albert Einstein, Martin Luther King, Jr., Helen Keller, and John Lasseter Can Teach You About Success and Fulfillment*

Take More Action and Increase Your Success and Feelings of Fulfillment:

- *Nothing Can Stop You This Year! How to Unleash Your Hidden Power to Persuade Well, Get More Done, Gain Sudden Profits, Command Intuition and Feel Great*

Increase Your Financial Abundance:

- *Love Yourself to Financial Abundance and Spiritual Joy: How You Can Remove Blocks to Your Prosperity, Happiness and Inner Peace*
- *Secrets of Rich, Smart and Powerful People: How You Can Use Leverage for Business Success*
- *10 Seconds to Wealth: Master the Moment Using Your Divine Gifts*
- *Truth No One Will Tell You: How to Feed Your Soul, Save a Business, or Get a Job During an Economic Crisis*
- *Full Strength Marketing: How You Can Use Your Hidden Strengths, Break through Inner Barriers and Raise Your Profits* (co-authored with Linda L. Chappo)

A Special Treat for Children, Parents and Grandparents:

- *Crystal Pegasus* (the graphic novel)

All books available at Amazon.com or BN.com (BarnesandNoble.com)

Special Offer to You, the reader

Contact tomsupercoach@gmail.com for a discount for private coaching, a workshop, *Top Five Group Elite Video Training* or a presentation (by Tom Marcoux) to your organization. Just mention your experience with this book. Thank you. The best to you.

www.ingramcontent.com/pod-product-compliance
Lightning Source LLC
LaVergne TN
LVHW050631100826
845148LV00011B/1823

* 9 7 8 0 6 1 5 9 2 8 6 9 2 *